# Science of Destiny Reading
## Using BaZi

Demystifying BaZi
the Logical Way

Authors: Gwan-Hwan Hwang Ph.D. /
Hsing-Fen Chiang

Translator: Richard Wang

Proofreaders: Paul Choo / Helen Yeh

# Contents

## Preface

**1**

Chapter

## Understanding BaZi with the Right Mindset     24

**2**

Chapter

## Real Cases of BaZi Analysis     32

# 3

Chapter

## The Basic Knowledge of BaZi     50

# 4 Dissecting the Intrinsic Personalities with the Four Pillars    102

Chapter

## 5

# 6

Chapter

## Taking Your BaZi Analysis Skills to the Next Level

280

# Preface

# Gwan-Hwan Hwang, Ph.D.

**Author**

- Professor and former chairman of the Department of Computer Science and Information Engineering, former vice dean of the College of Science, at National Taiwan Normal University
- Consultant for several cutting-edge technology companies in Taiwan
- Included in Marquis *Who's Who in Asia, in the World*, and in *Science and Engineering*

Even now, it is still very hard for me to believe that I am publishing a book about BaZi. As an engineer by training and an academic researcher for over 20 years, mastering BaZi was never part of my plan. When I first started years ago, all I wanted to find out was whether BaZi had any truth in it or was simply ancient baloney. I did not have any teachers to guide (or mislead) me. I studied everything on my own, with the same systematic method I used in my academic research work. In my career I have published many papers and professional articles but never a book addressed to the general public. Allow me to start by asking you to bear with me if in any part of this book the use of words is less than perfect.

Contrary to most of the books about fortune-telling, the main objective of this book is to help debunk superstitions. There are a lot of fortune-tellers who practice without trying to improve or even verify their own analyses. Whenever the result is not accurate, they conveniently attribute it to Karma or some sort of will of divinity. They are never wrong because they always say things that are ambiguous and unverifiable, with the sole purpose of scamming more money out of the client's pocket. Those who fall for their schemes often lose a lot more than just money. Some happy couples are torn apart. Others simply do not dare to enter relationships. Still others even send their children away for adoption because some fortune-teller told them that keeping their children in the family could threaten their own lives. All of these are undoubtedly superstitions, and should be condemned.

The art of fortune-telling, especially BaZi, was considered highly valuable in ancient China. Each school of practitioners guarded their knowledge as top secret. Many of them did so by spreading out false or misleading information so that they could keep the real knowledge within. This is why we are seeing so much false knowledge and superstition in the art of BaZi today. The only way to restore the knowledge to its purest essence is to study it with a scientific and logical attitude. I hope that this book can serve as a beginning to such an endeavor.

The influence of BaZi and the Five Elements to one's luck and life, although significant, is never absolute. Learning BaZi helps us understand the influence of the energies around us, but the purpose is to help us better plan our moves, not to make us submissive. We are still the masters of our lives. All we have to do is incorporate the influence of BaZi as we plan ahead and maintain a proactive attitude.

Learning BaZi not only gave me the ability to help others, but it also helped me develop a more open-minded and inclusive perspective of life. I became more interested in the topic of philosophy and life, and more willing to help others. I not only make constant charity donations from the income of my BaZi practice, but I also urge my clients to do the same.

I would like to thank my wife Hsin-Fen, who co-authored this book with me. Hsin-Fen has been my greatest help throughout the course of my BaZi study. She is a smart lady and a lot more sensitive in personal interactions than I am. Therefore, she can always provide me with valuable feedback. A lot of insights and findings that I developed came from her input. I always discuss every case with her.

Since the first Chinese edition was published, our readers have provided us with lots of positive feedback. Such recognition is the best reward and is what drives us forward. We have also received lots of questions from readers (prof.hwang.fortune.telling@gmail.com). We always reply to each one of them as best as we can. Many readers even visited us in person. Some of them came to Taiwan all the way from Hong Kong, Singapore, the United States, and Canada. I have always been moved to see them carrying copies of this book, which were filled with their notes and remarks on the pages. We really appreciate having such a group of supportive readers.

The basic principle of BaZi is simple, but applying it to real lives is a highly complicated art. I have the fortune to have a group of students who identify with my idea of studying BaZi from a scientific and logical perspective, and strengthened our course along the way. For that we are thankful.

This is our first English version. We made a lot of efforts to help English readers cross through the cultural barriers, which could have been the most difficult part for non-Chinese speakers to learn BaZi and perhaps the main reason that BaZi is less known outside Chinese society. We believe that the principle of BaZi can be learned across cultures and does not need to be lost in translation. With that in mind, we have made unprecedented changes, such as marking Heavenly Stems and Earthly Branches with simple symbols (H1–H12, E1–E12) instead of sticking to Chinese phonetic translations (Jia, Yi, Bing, Ding, etc.). We also translated the Ten Spirits with the same principle—making it easier to understand for English readers, rather than sticking to phonetics.

Another major effort we made in the English version is adding a number of case samples that are familiar to our English readers. The original Chinese version contains mostly examples of people in Taiwan. To better relate the art of BaZi to our English readers, we added a number of case studies of persons that would be familiar to English readers, such as Ernest Hemingway, Elizabeth Taylor, Michael Jordan, Vincent Van Gogh, and the recent presidential campaign in the United States (Trump vs. Clinton) and in France (Macron vs. Le Pen). We believe that these examples will bring the art of BaZi closer to our English speakers and prove that the principle of BaZi is universal.

We are excited to have this book published. We hope you will like our book and find the art of BaZi fascinating. We look forward to any feedback you may have.

# Preface

## Hsin-Fen Chiang

**Author**
- Bachelor of Arts, National Tsing-Hua University, Taiwan

I was exposed to fortune-telling since I was young. Many of my family members and distant relatives sought help from fortune-tellers of all schools, such as Zi-Wei-Dou-Shu (Chinese Astrology), face reading, palm reading, even the local temples with mediums. You name it, they mostly have tried it. Sometimes I went with them and observed the process. Whenever the fortune-teller told them that they are destined to have a rich and prosperous life, they were cheered and felt life full of hope. On the contrary, if the fortune-teller warns them that they will have trouble, lose their wealth or get sick, they got worried and depressed. If the warning is about their marriage, they got suspicious to their other halves and started to nose around, or even force their other half to vow for their loyalty. This sometimes ended up ruining their marriages (which ironically fulfilled the "prophecy"). Even worse, some of them believed in what the fortune-teller said and made aggressive investment, in the end losing all his retirement saving.

Having observed what happened to my relatives, I could not help but wonder why different fortune-tellers, based on the supposedly same school of technique (for example, BaZi), could derive such opposite conclusions? The same person could be judged to have a great life by one and to have a harsh life by another. For a while, I tried to understand the various theories behind the art of fortune-telling and bought some books to study. However, the more I read, the more confused I got. Not only did these books lack basic principle and logic, they were also full of special cases and exceptions. I finally gave up and stashed these books away. Perhaps fortune-telling is for someone more gifted than myself.

A few years ago, my husband brought home a few boxes of books about BaZi and started to study them in his leisure time. For a researcher in the technology field like himself, the inconsistencies and ambiguities that filled these books were really unbearable. He finally decided to get to the bottom of it. He started to analyze and compare all the books, weeding out the inconsistencies and controversial parts. Finally, he was able to build his model of modern BaZi theory around the main principle of yin and yang and the Five Elements. With that he started to verify and modify ideas based on real-life case studies through practice. This led to all that we present here in this book.

Modern BaZi theory extracts the real essence of BaZi from superstitions and folklore, making it a practice that could be applied to our daily lives. Each of us carries a combination of codes from the time of our births. The code combined with the Grand Fortune, Year Flow, and Month Flow, create a series of production and countering flow of energies that is unique to each individual and forms the pattern that affects a person's life. Knowing your own flow of energy can help you better understand who you are and build your plans accordingly. The flow of energy does not dictate what will happen to you but simply tells you who you are and how you could best plan your life. It helps you better choose your career, plan your investments, do the right things at the right time, manage your relationships in the way that best fit you. It is not a superstition but a tool that you can use to gain control of your life.

I am thankful to be part of the BaZi research of my husband, who has the patience and interest to study BaZi in a logical and systematic way. It has been a rewarding and memorable experience to study and discuss all the cases with him. I am also very thankful to my friends and family, who have openly shared their life experiences to help us verify and improve our practices.

Since the first edition in Chinese was published in 2013, we received tremendous feedback and acknowledgement around the world. Along with them came hundreds of cases for us to further test our theory, making it even more solid. For that I can't appreciate enough all of those readers who have supported us.

We cherish each person that is brought to us on the path of studying BaZi. Studying with friends who share this interest is always pleasant. I invite you all to join our journey and move forward together.

# Preface

## Richard Wang

**Translator**
- Master's degree in Engineering, University of Texas; MBA, Santa Clara University
- Business and venture capital professional
- A disciple of Professor Gwan-Hwan Hwang

Any study of natural phenomena starts with observing and recording, followed by building a hypothesis with a model that can logically explain the phenomena. The modeled hypothesis then has to be subject to extensive experiments and verifications from all parties before it can be widely accepted as a theory. Any person who has basic training of science should be familiar with this process.

However, as we get accustomed to taking what we learned in school for granted, we often forget that all the scientific theories we treat as truth were at one point hypotheses, and many of them were highly controversial at the time. Some of them were even rejected by mainstream society. It took decades or even generations of relentless study and debates before they became accepted.

I was raised in a church-going family and studied engineering in college. With my upbringing, I have always regarded any form of fortune-telling as superstition, a scam used to trick less educated people. As I grew older and experienced more, I started to realize that not everything in life can be explained logically, and I began to wonder whether there was some other invisible force at play. For a while, I tried to be open-minded and study what fortune-telling was, but my short-lived journey soon became a frustrating one. With the books I read and classes I attended, not a single one offered a convincing theory. They either consisted of hundreds of rules that had no logical connections between them, or they simply resorted to some sort of divine power and hence should not be questioned. My brain is simply not built for studying things without any logic behind them. Maybe I am simply not gifted enough to master such "divine knowledge"?

In 2017, I had the fortune to read the book of Professor Hwang. The book quickly became an eye-opener, for it was the first book about fortune-telling that made sense to me. I quickly studied it all and started to learn BaZi personally under Professor Hwang. Soon I felt everything came together. Alas! The BaZi and the principle of the Five Elements were actually the hypothesis and models built by our ancestors, after having observed the phenomena and events around them. This is actually a model with its own theory, a model that explains how it works, and it can be researched and verified. Professor Hwang, after years of study, dusted away the superstitions and falsehood that had covered it over the past thousand years, and restored it to its original state. BaZi is no longer something dominated by "divine power," but rather a scientific theory like any other that can be studied logically.

Moreover, based on Professor Hwang's BaZi theory, the power of the universal energies in our lives is just like the weather around us. It could be obvious but never absolute. One's life is never destined. If the weather forecast says a storm is approaching, it simply tells you to be prepared by checking the roof or bringing an umbrella if you need to go out. It would be a bit insane if you believed that you are destined to get soaked. The same logic applies to BaZi. Studying it does not make people passive and succumb to "the inevitable." On the contrary, it is a way for us to proactively understand our lives and try to make better use of it.

Compared to today, in ancient times society was a lot simpler and more closed. People's lives were easier to observe. For those who wanted to study the forces that interacted with people's lives, ancient society provided a much better opportunity that is similar to the "lab environment." Maybe this is why our ancestors were able to deduce a theory like BaZi. If we could study it with the right attitude, I believe it would be of tremendous value, for it can help us see who we are and improve our lives.

# Preface

## Paul Choo

**Proofreader**
- Singaporean
- Finance Professional in Singapore
- A disciple of Professor Gwan-Hwan Hwang

I cannot recall how many books I have read on the subject of BaZi. Being Singaporean and English educated, it has not been easy to find good English books on BaZi. A lot of books on this subject were written by Taiwanese and Hong Kong masters; however, without proper guidance, most of the writings were either too difficult to understand or had very little practical application.

Anyone who has embarked on the journey to learn BaZi would have come across the concept of "favourable gods" ( 喜神 ) and "unfavourable gods" ( 忌神 ). The toughest part of the learning process is to figure out which element is favourable and which unfavourable. Figuring this out is only half the problem; the other issue is deriving consistency from the readings. Very few books can give you the answer to the above problem and, in most cases, the theories contradict one another.

Professor Hwang's book brings a breath of fresh air to all the titles I have read. It is by far, the easiest to understand and the most comprehensive book I have come across. Anyone who has some basic knowledge of BaZi will find the concepts presented in this book easy to understand. What sets this book apart from the rest is that it does away with the concept of strong and weak chart, and focuses mainly on the 10 gods, 5 elements, heavenly stem combo and earthly branch 6 combo. The rules are clear and there is no ambiguity in how they are applied in chart reading. No book on the market has been able to clearly explain how to do readings on a month-to-month basis. I wish I had this book when I started learning BaZi. If there is only one book you ever need to learn on this subject, this would be it. I look forward to the day that this book is translated to English and more people can enjoy this wonderful book.

# Preface

## Julian Lee

- Singaporean
- Finance Professional In Singapore
- A disciple of Professor Gwan-Hwan Hwang

I first "encountered" Professor Hwang's BaZi book when I was in Taiwan, together with my BaZi buddies a couple of years ago. Because I had been learning about BaZi for some time and become close to several BaZi enthusiasts in Singapore and Malaysia, I was extremely interested in getting to know new perspectives of BaZi, to the extent of being "obsessed" with decoding our destinies through the BaZi charts.

The BaZi book you are now reading is very unique for our time. Many books have been written on the subject of BaZi. Of those, most are superficial, force-feeding information to readers and with little analytical consistency.

Professor Hwang's BaZi book sets a new standard for the BaZi community and for writers around the world in terms of conveying simple BaZi concepts to his readers. The book also attests to the fact that real art was never meant to be complicated.

I wish I had met Professor Hwang much earlier in my life, but then again it is never too late to find the real meaning of BaZi accuracy. I hope Professor Hwang's book will eventually be translated into English so that many more readers can appreciate what our forefathers have left for us in this world.

Lastly, it is the duty of those of us here today to preserve in accurate detail the art of BaZi reading and how the destiny chart can be accurately decoded, especially for future generations. Professor Hwang has done well for BaZi communities around the world in this respect.

# Chapter 1

## Understanding BaZi with the Right Mindset

In modern society, most people who consider themselves well educated do not easily believe in fortune-telling. Many simply disregard it as superstition, or worse yet, as a scam designed to skim money off those who fall for it. Indeed, such scams do exist in all societies, and once in a while we read about them.

I also consider myself an educated person and a man of science. I received an advanced degree in science and engineering from a top university in Taiwan, and I have been a faculty member of a national university. For over a decade, I have taught classes in the field of engineering, led research labs, published papers in most reputable international journals, and advised many Ph.D. student.

Because of that, when my wife sought the consultation of BaZi fortune-telling years ago, it was hard for me to take it seriously. Nevertheless, some of the analysis appeared to check out. This made me wonder whether BaZi, being the most popular and widely accepted form of fortune-telling in Chinese society, could have some truth behind it. Out of curiosity, I started to collect all the material on BaZi I could find and began to study them. Aside from my work, I spent a lot of time gathering and comparing information from different schools of BaZi practitioners. I cross-checked their theories against real case samples, in hopes to reveal any real essence that is hidden beneath layers of myths and superstitions.

The art of BaZi analysis developed over the course of hundreds of years. Practitioners learned what they knew as an apprentice from their masters. Few of those practitioners had any academic training in logic and science. Therefore, most of the theories on the market are not only fragmented but also illogical. But after years of study, I was able to derive a BaZi system that I am convinced to be not only logical but also applicable to almost all scenarios. With that, I am also able to explain why some schools of BaZi practitioners, with their traditional teachings, could be accurate in some cases while totally off the mark in others.

Unlike most of the traditional methods that have been passed down for generations with no logic or theory behind them, the BaZi analysis I developed follows a systematic and logical approach. Through years of personal practice, I am convinced that the system I have developed can and have indeed been quite accurate. Some may challenge that without total accuracy and a scientific way of measurement, this cannot be trusted as a meaningful indication. But many natural phenomena were observed by our ancestors long before scientists could have measured them. Furthermore, even with modern technology, meteorologists still cannot be completely accurate in forecasting the weather just 10 days in advance. The course of a person's life lasts decades and can be affected by so many factors (genes, education, environment, and so on). To expect that we can use a single factor to predict outcomes is probably not practical. However, if a systematic method can indeed tell a person's character, as well as the relative ups and downs throughout their life, it is, in my opinion, something worth studying. The BaZi analytic system that I have developed is, through my practice with hundreds of cases, a system that does just that.

## The Limitations of the Traditional BaZi Methods

Through my research, I have realized that each traditional BaZi school has its limitations and blind spots. This is not to say that mine is flawless (in fact, I believe that there is always room in my system for improvement). The point is that, with a modern education and training in analytic thinking, we should be able to study BaZi from a new perspective that is much different from traditional rules and methods.

The traditional way of learning BaZi requires memorizing some tables and rules. These tables and rules are not only hard to memorize but also illogical. Furthermore, each table and rule has cases of exceptions, which require further memorization. During my study of BaZi, I found that this was the case for most books and scripts on BaZi, including the ancient and most famous ones.

Such a method of rote memorization might have been the best way of passing on knowledge in the past, when people rarely received any training in science and logic. The problem, however, is that those trained under such systems could only deal with cases that they were taught. They could not handle cases that they were not taught. Also, as most of the knowledge was acquired through memorization, any piece of information that was incorrectly memorized would also be passed on. This is why the traditional BaZi methods can only be partly accurate in some cases.

My system, on the contrary, was developed purely around the fundamental principle of yin-yang and the interrelationship among the Five Elements. With a few simple and logical rules, we can derive all we need to know. Since we derive our results through logical analysis, as opposed to the old-school method of looking up tables, there is no exceptional case or case not covered. With our analytical method, we can even tell under what scenarios the traditional methods will miss the mark.

I do not intend to criticize the works of our ancestors. In fact, it is because of their work that my study became possible. But I do believe that we should not dwell on the old approach, which was developed with the limitations of the past that are no longer relevant. The lack of consistent logic indeed made the old approach less accurate and invites suspicion among those in modern society.

# Our Vision

The prevalence of information on the Internet has made research on BaZi so much easier these years. Unlike practitioners in the past who had to rely on cases of people close by, those who study BaZi today have access to a lot more information and to cases from around the world. They can study celebrities' life events on the news. With a systematic approach, this enables one to more efficiently refine the theory of BaZi, weeding out myths and misconceptions quickly.

That said, I still come across a lot of illogical or wrong information about BaZi on the Internet. Some information can be ridiculously wrong. This is probably why some people have dismissed the theory of BaZi as baloney, a cheap trick to sell snake oil. Fortunately, throughout the years of my practice, I have helped many people learn the theory I have developed. Most people I helped came to respect BaZi as a serious art of destiny reading.

Unlike some practitioners who judge their clients' fate as absolute, the way I practice is simply to help my clients make informed decisions. These include reminding them to be cautious when there are hazards ahead, encouraging them when they are at low points in their lives by showing them the light at the end of the tunnel, advising them whether the timing is good for being on the offensive or defensive. I practiced based on the system I developed and conducted counseling sessions over one-to-one conversations. I was able to win their trust by telling them things that have happened in their lives, and further removed their worries and confusions by pointing out situations ahead.

The more I study and practice, the more I am convinced that BaZi is a serious subject, discovered by our ancestors and passed down to us. It is a valuable asset worthy of further research and study. It is my vision that someday BaZi will no longer be treated as a myth but recognized as a valuable method that helps improve people's lives. The goal of this book is to convey four core principles for those who are interested in studying BaZi:

- Study it from a logical perspective
- Remove myths and extract real knowledge
- Help people deal with their troubles
- Improve lives

The knowledge passed on by the ancient books is not all false. In fact, it contains all the gems of the essence of BaZi, based on which we can build on what we know. But over the course of centuries, real knowledge is inevitably mixed with, or worse, buried under a lot of false information. I hope that with the modern method of systematic research, we can to the greatest extent restore BaZi to the way it should be.

In this book, we will introduce the knowledge of BaZi in the following order:

- **Chapter 2:** Present real cases to illustrate how BaZi can be applied in real life, and in what way it can help people.

- **Chapter 3:** Introduce the basic elements on which the system of BaZi is constructed, such as the Five Elements, the Heavenly Stems and Earthly Branches, the twelve Solar Terms, and the Ten Spirits.

- **Chapter 4:** Show readers how to conduct a basic analysis of BaZi to judge an individual's basic personality and characteristics, as well as their strengths, weaknesses, best-fit careers, and health conditions.

- **Chapter 5:** Illustrate how to put the BaZi of a person together with his Grand Fortune, the Year Flow, and Month Flow to analyze luck during different periods of life, and use the information to seize opportunities or avoid hazards.

- **Chapter 6:** Present more advanced topics that help readers further strengthen their BaZi analytic skills. Those who wish to use BaZi to help others should learn this.

- **Chapter 7:** Discuss some commonly seen theories of traditional BaZi, and how and why they can be inaccurate.

- **Chapter 8:** Share a few tips with those who want to practice BaZi counseling. The conducts that should be adopted as well as the mental qualities required to be a good practitioner.

# Chapter 2

# Real Cases of
# BaZi Analysis

efore we introduce the theory of BaZi, we will present a few real cases of BaZi analysis in this chapter. I have accumulated hundreds of case studies from my consulting practice in the past years, but I chose these cases as they are more representative for the purpose of learning BaZi. Here, in this chapter, I will present only the cases and the results. In Chapter 5, we will revisit each case and understand how we arrived at the conclusions of the analyses. Readers who study this book carefully will be able to solve similar cases in the future.

## Case Study 1
## Ankylosing spondylitis

One day, in 2012, I was having a casual conversation with one of my graduate students. He mentioned that he did not have to serve in the military (one-year military service is mandatory for all males in Taiwan, unless one is physically or mentally unfit for such duty). I was curious and asked him why. He told me that he was suffering from ankylosing spondylitis.

As a BaZi practitioner, I was intrigued. I suspected that his ankylosing spondylitis should have something to do with countered Wood in his BaZi, and I asked for his birth date and time to build his BaZi chart, which was just as I had expected. I then asked him if he has had any serious conditions in the past two years (2010 and 2011). He immediately said yes. Although he showed no symptoms in 2012, he did suffer severely in 2011 and 2010, during which years he was also under tremendous pressure from his then supervising professor.

This is very obvious on his BaZi chart. Whenever H7 or H8 appears on his Heavenly Stem side, he is likely to suffer the syndrome. With that, I told him not to worry too much over the next few years, but to pay attention to those years ending with 0 or 1 (e.g., 2020 and 2021). Also, during the month of H7 or H8, he may also feel some minor discomfort.

From a different perspective, his short-term adverse physical condition saved him one year of military service. This might not have been such a bad thing after all.

# Case Study 2
# The affair of Chien-Min Wang

Chien-Min Wang is famous in Taiwan for being among the first Taiwanese baseball players who made it to the US Major League. His love affair that broke out in the media in 2010 caught a lot of public attention and dented his image quite a bit. Wang's birthdate is March 31, 1980. There are a few versions of his birth time on the Internet. Based on the known events, we think the hour of E11 is the most likely birth time.

According to the press, Wang started having the affair in 2010. The affair lasted eight months. In April 2012 the affair was somehow exposed to the public. These series of events could be explained based on his BaZi chart.

Based on his BaZi chart, I believe that Wang is not someone who lacks moral values or a sense of responsibility. As a fan of his, I sincerely hope that he can soon walk away from this temporary low point in his life and return to his former glory.

# Case Study 3
# No one believed what I said

In 2010, I had an opportunity to reunite with two of my college classmates. More than twenty years after college, they were both very accomplished, with their own companies. It goes without saying that we were all excited with our reunion and had a great time together. During our casual conversation, one of the classmates mentioned that he had a problem with his kidney. Almost out of intuition I responded, "Let me guess. It was severe two years ago, but it's fine this year." He was very surprised, as that was indeed the case. I told him that I was studying BaZi and added, "I bet that there is Earth countering Water in your BaZi chart. If not, the dinner is on me." His birth date and time was December 7, 1964, at the hour of E4. I quickly built his BaZi chart, which showed exactly what I expected.

The year 2009 was the year of H6-E2. The energy of Earth was heavy on both Heavenly Stem and Earthly Branch. It's not a surprise that Earth countered Water and triggered issues with his kidney. Throughout 2010 and 2011 his kidney did not bother him. One day, in 2012, however, while I dropped by his office for our appointment, he was absent. His colleagues told me that he called in sick, as his kidney problem had reoccurred. Whenever this happened, his whole body gets swollen, and this time was no exception.

I immediately checked his BaZi chart against the Month Flow, and told his colleagues that this time the cause was not the kidney, but more likely the liver, gallbladder, or immune system. From the perplexed expressions of his colleagues, no one seemed to believe what I said. A few days later when he returned to work, he told his colleagues that he has been taking steroid for years to control his kidney problem, and as a result, he had problems with his immune system. Again, the expressions of his colleagues upon hearing this was priceless.

I also advised him that his kidney problem would likely reoccur after April, 2012, and hoped that he could follow the doctor's instructions and take good care of his health.

# Case Study 4
# Never judge a person by appearance

I don't remember all the details of this case, but these are two things that I remember quite vividly. One day, a team of young men and women who all worked in the same technology company came to seek my consultation. A slim, delicate looking young lady asked a few questions regarding her relationship with her boyfriend. Before I even checked her Grand Fortune, and Year and Month Flow, I asked her directly "Are you having trouble with your boyfriend because of your temper?" Her colleagues were not convinced, as she did not appear to be a girl with a temper. To their surprise, however, she said, "Yes." I then analyzed how her relationship might have been in the past six months, based on her BaZi. She felt that it was quite consistent with what she experienced, and therefore, asked for further advice over the following months.

The woman also told me that she had had surgery in 2009 and asked me whether there could be any side effects in the future. Without knowing the details of the surgery, I first analyzed her BaZi in 2009. It seemed that the surgery was most likely performed in June, July, or August, and should be something related to countered Fire. Before I asked her for further details, she told me it was an eye surgery. I immediately replied, "if the surgery was not on both eyes, then it should have been the left eye." She said, "How could you know this?" The entire audience was shocked.

Frankly speaking, just by looking at her, it was almost impossible to take her as someone with a temper, and her eyes did not seem to have any problems. So how could we uncover what is hidden and use what we know to help the person?

One additional note—some conventional BaZi practitioners use the theory of "Bodily Strong" and "Bodily Weak" to analyze one's fortune. According to this theory, those who are "Bodily Strong" have good fortune under the energy of Officers. My own BaZi is also considered "Bodily Strong." According to the theory I should have been doing pretty well when I was under the Fortune of Officers. But in reality, I was having big trouble with my eyes during that period and had surgery. It was hardly a good fortune.

If we simply analyze using the basic principle of the Five Elements, we will see that those who are categorized under "Bodily Strong" do have a higher chance of seeing good fortune under the energy of Officer. But this is not always the case. This is why the practitioners who rely on this theory tend to reach incorrect conclusions from time to time.

# Case Study 5
# Confidential matters that are not known to family members

In my experience, sometimes providing consultation to someone you know is a lot harder than to a total stranger. My wife has a family member who, for a while, was not doing too well. Her family asked me to take a look at his BaZi and see if there is any advice I can provide. He was born on July 12, 1973, at the hour of E10. With his BaZi chart laid out, the first thing I noticed was severe Officer countering Self in 2009 between September and November. To my surprise, the reply I got from the family member was that nothing happened during that period. I was quite puzzled. Based on the chart, even if nothing happened, at least he would have been under a lot of pressure during the period.

A few months later, that same family member tried to borrow some money from the family and told them that he was having litigation problems due to copyright infringement.

He had to pay a penalty of US$50,000. It turned out that the litigation did take place during the period I enquired about earlier. He did not tell me about this, as he did not want his family to know about it.

With that, I re-examined his BaZi. The Officer countering Peer was also present in 2005. From what I was told, it was the year when he started his career in China, and he was having a hard time dealing with his boss. That said, the worst time should have be over after 2009. His BaZi showed that he should be doing a lot better in 2010 and 2011.

Another case that I had involved a friend of mine. Once he asked me about his opportunities with women. I pointed out a possible month in the recent past, and he denied seeing anyone during that period. After a while, he admitted to me in private that he did have a relationship, which, for some reason, needed to be kept private. He had denied it when I asked him about it because there were other friends there.

With experiences like these, nowadays in my consulting session, I always ask to be alone with the client. And I would always start by assuring my client that all our conversation remains confidential.

# Case Study 6
# In memory of Echo

One Saturday afternoon in 2012, I took my wife on a scenic ride in the mountains of Hsinchu. We drove all the way to the village of Qinchuan. Other than the famous residence of late General Chang Xue-Liang, we visited the residence of Echo (1943–1991), also known as San Mao, a famous Taiwanese writer who had committed suicide. Although we had read quite a lot of her works, we did not know a lot about her life until the visit to her residence that day.

As is the habit of a BaZi practitioner, I wondered how her BaZi looked. My first intuition was that with her talents and the works she created, the Creation element must be strong in her BaZi. But she did not get along well with her teachers (Note 1), and was very unfortunate in her marriage (Note 2). Both are indications of Creation countering Officer. Furthermore, her suffering from depression in her last years could be a sign of Empowerment countering Creation. It got so serious that she took her own life. I assume there was no Peer that helped bridge the countering.

That night I looked up Echo's birth date and time. March 26, 1943 at the hour of E3. The BaZi showed just what I had expected. Both Main Creation and Side Creations are rooted. Among the eight elements, Creation occupied four. Furthermore, two Side Officers sat next to Main Creation, inviting a direct countering. In my experience, females with strong Creation and no Wealth in the BaZi charts normally do not have good fortune when it comes to marriage. I know a lady who is very successful in her career but was still single at the age of 50. Her BaZi also shows such a pattern.

Echo's BaZi shows her path of life, such as the timing that her creations (her literary works) caught public attention, the death of her beloved husband, and her symptoms of depression that eventually took her life.

Note 1: She was publicly humiliated once in middle school, which traumatized her and led to her dropping out of school.

Note 2: She had three major relationships in which she was either married or about to get married, but all ended tragically. In the first one, she was ready to enter into marriage, despite opposition from her family, but later discovered that her fiancé was already married. In the second one, her fiancé died of a heart attack while they were preparing for their wedding. The third major relationship and only marriage was with José María Quero Y Ruíz, a Spanish national. They lived happily in the Sahara Desert and the Canary Islands but José died in a diving accident in 1979, five years after their marriage. According to the memoir of Echo's sister, Echo was so devastated that she tried to dig José's grave with her bare hands.

# Case Study 7
# It happened anyway

The client is a friend of my wife's. She was born on May 11, 1976, at the hour of E7. Self is H10. Other than that, the Heavenly Stem of her BaZi chart has only Wealth. Such a chart is very simple to analyze. Whenever Side Officer is present with no Creation or Empowerment, accidents or bad things are prone to occur. In her case, it could also imply that during such a period she may be subject to physical conditions related to countered Water, such as kidney or bladder problems.

In 2008, her Grand Fortune switched to Side Officer after April. Hence, I gave her a call to remind her to be careful, and it turned out that she had just been admitted to hospital for a kidney problem. Similar episodes happened a few times afterward. She visited hospital just shortly before or after my call. For a while, I was a bit worried that she thought of me as a bad omen.

At the beginning of 2010, she called me for a consultation as she was thinking of having a baby. She had had a daughter in the spring of 2008, and now she wanted to have another child. I did not spend a lot of time addressing her potential for getting pregnant. Instead I reminded her to be careful at the end of 2010 and the beginning of 2011. Most practitioners would think that 2010 would have been good timing for her, as it was the year of H7-E3, and E3 is Creation for her. But throughout that year she was not able to conceive.

In December, 2010, she called my wife to say that she was finally pregnant. My wife asked me to review her BaZi chart again. I looked at her chart for a long time without saying a word. My wife got quite nervous and asked me if there was anything wrong. I told her that all I could say was that I honestly was not sure why she got pregnant now, and she needed to be very, very careful in January in matters relating to accidents, injuries, pressure, or other adverse conditions.

A few days later, my wife was informed that her friend had gone to the hospital and found out that her baby did not have a heartbeat. As a result, she had to have surgery to abort the baby, which did take place in January. Fortunately, the surgery went well, and she came out all right. Surgery is one possible manifestation of Side Officer countering Self. But this was quite a dramatic episode.

She then conceived again during June/July of 2011. This time I expected she should be able to get through safely, and indeed she had no problem this time.

In February 2017, we were informed that she had gotten pregnant again. I again checked her BaZi and found a serious Empowerment countering Creation. I informed her to pay attention and get a lot of rest. Unfortunately, in March the doctor again diagnosed that the baby's heart had stopped beating, and she had to have an abortion.

# Case Study 8
# Recovery from cancer

A client of mine who worked in a reputable high-tech company referred his brother to me for consultation. His brother had nasopharyngeal cancer. They wanted to know if his condition would improve. I analyzed and told them that the condition should soon improve. A few months later, I was told that the chemotherapy was quite successful. The client was able to recover and go back to work again.

Another similar case regarded a distant relative of mine. He was in his sixties. The cancer had been with him for over a decade and eventually spread to his bones. At the time, I analyzed that his cancer should have been caused by his blood, and that his condition should improve. I was not sure if anyone in his family believed what I said. After all, it would be pretty hard to believe that someone with his age and with cancer already spread to the bone could recover.

A few years later, I heard that the old gentleman did recover and had returned home. He was not only able to take care of himself but sometimes even helped pick up his grandson from school. I was also told that soon after my consultation, his family had gone to a local temple and received an answer from a psychic similar to what I had told them. Since I know nothing about religion and the spiritual world, I will just leave it as a surprising coincidence.

I would like to make it clear that, BaZi analysis cannot and shall not in any way replace medical treatment. Both clients in these case studies received formal medical treatment in regular hospitals.

## Case Study 9
## Should you take the role of CEO?

This case is about an information technology company founded by a group of young entrepreneurs from a top university in Taiwan. The company had been growing its business nicely and was planning to go IPO. At the beginning of 2012, the family members of the client (born on March 16, 1973, at the hour of E6) visited me. Without giving me any information, they asked: "how is his fortune this year?" I said, "Officer produces Empowerment. Looks like he will have the good fortune of getting a promotion or rising to power." It turned out my answer was a spot on. The client was working in the company we mentioned. The board invited him to take the role of CEO. But he felt that it was a big organization with many people who had more experience than him. He felt a bit troubled, as he was not sure whether he should accept such big responsibility.

Based on his BaZi, I was convinced that his fortune relating to his career was on an unstoppable rise since early 2012. A few days later, I talked to the client over the phone and advised that he should boldly take the opportunity. To further convince him, I analyzed his fortune in the past years, and it was quite consistent with what I had predicted. He eventually took the CEO position.

Analyzing what happened in the past is a very powerful tool to convince clients. Once the client is convinced, they will be more open to our consultation. But such a tool in the wrong hands can be easily used to manipulate clients for one's own interests. This is why BaZi practitioners in the past were very selective in choosing disciples with high ethical standards. That said, most people seek help because they are anxious about the uncertainty of the future. If we use the tool properly, we can help our client face the future with more confidence.

# Case Study 10
# Accidents that happened to me and my student

Being a BaZi practitioner does not mean that I am above the law of nature. As a matter of fact, in my BaZi chart my Self is H3 of Fire. In June 2012 (year H9-E5, month H3-E7), the water of H9 countered the Fire of H3. For those with H3 as Self, this month the Side Officer of H9 countered Self. Unless there is Earth countering Water or Wood bridging the countering, this month could be dangerous. (Note: readers should not be intimidated by the terms in this paragraph. All of this will be explained in chapters 3–5.)

As I knew about this, I went to donate blood in hope of directing the bad energy. The donation went rather well, but after the donation was complete, the blood vessel was not properly pressurized and, as a result, it created a large bruise on my arm. I told myself that if this was the fulfillment of the Side Officer countering Self, then I was rather lucky that it did not manifest into something worse. I am a person that believes in good Karma. I always donate a portion of my consulting income to charity. Maybe the good Karma saved me from more severe situations.

In the same month, I was informed that a thesis coauthored by myself and one of my Ph.D. students had just been accepted for publication in a journal. My student had already started to work in a company but needed this to complete his Ph.D. degree, so I reached out to him immediately. While on the phone with him, I recalled that he also has Self of H3 as myself. I looked at the bruise on my forearm and casually asked how he has been doing. He told me that he just had surgery.

I asked him if the surgery took place around late May or early June. He confirmed that was the case. I then asked if it had something to do with his eyes or intestines (as will be covered later, issues related to the eyes and intestine are often seen with countered Fire). He told me it was his intestine. Luckily, the surgery was a success. He also told me that he had accidentally cut his finger a few days ago and had a few stitches. I told him not to worry too much, as things would get better after this month.

With the above examples, readers should have an appreciation of how BaZi can be used to help us avoid bad things that could happen in our lives, or at least reduce their impact.

# Chapter 3

# The Basic Knowledge
# of BaZi

In this chapter, we will introduce the basic elements that constitute the theory of BaZi. In Section 1, we will introduce the Five Elements, the very foundation of BaZi. Section 2 covers the Heavenly Stems (天干 *tian-gan*) and Earthly Branches (地支 *di-zhi*), followed by the twelve solar terms of the year in Section 3. In Section 4, we will use all of the above to build a BaZi chart.

Once a chart is built, we will be able to derive the Ten Spirits in Section 5. In Section 6, we will discuss the structure (格局 *ge-ju*) of a chart. Last but not least, in Section 7 we will cover other types of important interactions among the Five Elements. The information provided in this chapter will prepare us for analyzing a person's character and personality based on their BaZi chart.

# Section 1
# The Five Elements

Most Chinese are familiar with the Five Elements. For those who are new to this, the Five Elements are wood (木 *mu*), fire (火 *huo*), earth (土 *tu*), metal (金 *jin*), and water (水 *shui*). Ancient Chinese believed that these Five Elements are the essences that form all materials in the universe. For the purpose of learning BaZi, we may simply think of them as five different types of energies (氣 *qi*) that emerge and dissipate periodically as the result of the periodical movements among the earth, the sun, and the universe. Also, each person, based on their time of birth, can be represented by a unique composition of the Five Elements.

The energies of the Five Elements, when interacting with one another, can cause effects of production (相生 *xiang sheng*), or countering (相剋 *xiang ke*). When the energy of one element "produces" the energy of another element, the former enhances, or transfers, its energy to the other element, making the latter element stronger. On the other hand, when the energy of one element "counters" the energy of another element, that means the former suppresses or inhibits the latter, thereby weakening the latter's power.

To make it easier for our readers to remember and take notes, we will use the following abbreviations to represent the Five Elements: "V" for wood (with the letter V from the word Vegetation in order to differentiate it from the "water"); "F" for fire; "E" for earth, "M" for metal, and "W" for water.

Figure 1 shows the relationship between production and countering among the energies of the Five Elements. The solid lines with circles represent the relationships of production. The dotted lines with crosses represent countering relationships. We memorize the five elements in the order of wood, fire, earth, metal, water, as wood produces fire, fire produces earth, earth produces metal, metal produces water, and water produces wood. Any two elements would either produce or counter each other.

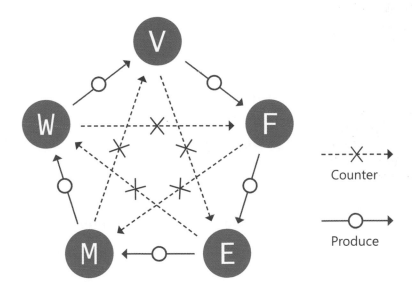

**Figure 1:** The relationships of production and countering among the energies of the Five Elements

# Production

To help us memorize the relationships of production amongst the Five Elements, we could use the following visualization tips, as shown in Table 1.

**Table 1:** Visualization tips for production amongst the Five Elements

| | |
|---|---|
| **Wood produces fire** | Visualize building a fire with wood. |
| **Fire produces earth** | Visualize the fire producing ash (soil). |
| **Earth produces metal** | Visualize metal being mined from the ground (earth). |
| **Metal produces water** | Visualize metal melting into liquid before being cast into a tool. |
| **Water produces wood** | Visualize water irrigating trees. |

# Countering

To help memorize the relationship of countering energies, readers may use the visualization tips provided in the following table:

**Table 2:** Visualization tips for countering of the Five Elements

| | |
|---|---|
| **Wood counters earth** | Visualize the roots of a tree grabbing onto the earth. |
| **Earth counters water** | Visualize a dike or dam built by earth to contain water. |
| **Water counters fire** | Visualize water putting out fire. |
| **Fire counters metal** | Visualize fire melting metal. |
| **Metal counters wood** | Visualize an ax made of metal chopping down a tree. |

Please note that the visualization tips are only to help readers memorize the interactions between the Five Elements. Readers should not ascribe too much meaning to them.

Many people would ask me "how can one prove that the energies of the Five Elements exist?" Some would argue that BaZi theory does not merit any serious discussion unless one can clearly prove where the energies of the Five Elements come from.

But in fact, throughout the history of modern science, many hypotheses have been made, and scientific models were built much longer before their existence could be proven. For example, the existence of electrons was theorized way before scientists could observe it. Scientists discovered the characteristics of such elements through observation and experiments and made hypotheses accordingly. Such a cycle of observation—hypothesis—validation exists in almost every major field of science, and the same thought process should also be applied to the art of destiny reading.

Since physics is not my specialty, I would probably not have the opportunity to investigate the very source of the Five Elements. But validating BaZi case after case using the principle of the Five Elements is, to me, pretty much like validating the existence of the Five Elements. The effects of the Five Elements can indeed be observed through the ups and downs of a person's life. I believe that any person with a real mind for science and logic would not just reject it blindly.

By the same token, the Heavenly Stems and Earthly Branches that we are about to discuss in the next section also cannot yet be concretely proven by modern science. But we should treat it as something derived from and hypothesized by ancient people through diligent observations of nature throughout the generations.

# Section 2
# The Ten Heavenly Stems (*tian gan*) and the Twelve Earthly Branches (*di zhi*)

The Heavenly Stems and the Earthly Branches are traditionally used by Chinese to count years. In fact, month, day, and even hour can also be represented by the combination of them. For example, the 1st of June, 2012, would be year *ren-chen*, month *yi-si*, day *gui-si*. Don't panic if you have no idea what we are talking about. We are about to cover it.

## The Ten Heavenly Stems
## (天干 *tian gan*)

The Ten Heavenly Stems are *jia, yi, bing, ding, wu, ji, geng, xin, ren, gui*. Each stem has its attribute of the Five Elements, as well as yin (positive) and yang (negative).

To save our English readers from the excruciating process of memorizing these Chinese characters, in this book we will simply use symbols H1 to H10 to represent the ten Heavenly Stems.

Table 3 summarizes the Heavenly Stems and their attributes. We use symbol '+' to represent yang and '–' to represent yin.

**Table 3:** The Ten Heavenly Stems

| Symbol | Name | Attribute | Visualization tip |
|--------|------|-----------|-------------------|
| H1 | 甲 (*jia*) | V+ | Big tree |
| H2 | 乙 (*yi*) | V− | Grass |
| H3 | 丙 (*bing*) | F+ | Sun |
| H4 | 丁 (*ding*) | F− | Candle light |
| H5 | 戊 (*wu*) | E+ | Heavy rock |
| H6 | 己 (*ji*) | E− | Soft soil |
| H7 | 庚 (*geng*) | M+ | Sword |
| H8 | 辛 (*xin*) | M− | Jewel |
| H9 | 壬 (*ren*) | W+ | Ocean |
| H10 | 癸 (*gui*) | W− | Mist |

A common mistake made by beginners of BaZi is to mix up yin and yang. This may cause serious error in the result of the analysis. Do try to remember the elements and the yin-yang attribute of each stem, and carefully apply them when analyzing a BaZi chart.

## The Twelve Earthly Branches (地支 *di zhi*)

The Twelve Earthly Branches are *zi, chou, yin, mao, chen, si, wu, wei, shen, you, xu, hai.* Again, to simplify the learning process, we will represent them with symbols E1 to E12 in this book (Table 4).

The Earthly Branches are more complicated. Each branch also has its element and yin-yang attribute, as shown in the table below. For example, E1 (*zi*) is yin Water (W−).

But other than the main energy, most Earthly Branches contain one or more visible energies. This is called "hidden stem(s)." It is believed that the energy of an Earthly Branch is composed of more than one of the Five Elements (see column 4 of the table).

**Table 4:** The Twelve Earthly Branches

| Symbol | Name | Attribute | Hidden Stems | Zodiac | Hour | Month |
|--------|------|-----------|--------------|--------|------|-------|
| E1 | 子 (*zi*) | W– | H10 | Rat | 23:00–00:59 | December |
| E2 | 丑 (*chou*) | E– | H6, H8, H10 | Ox | 01:00–02:59 | January |
| E3 | 寅 (*yin*) | V+ | H1, H3, H5 | Tiger | 03:00–04:59 | February |
| E4 | 卯 (*mao*) | V– | H2 | Rabbit | 05:00–06:59 | March |
| E5 | 辰 (*chen*) | E+ | H5, H10, H2 | Dragon | 07:00–08:59 | April |
| E6 | 巳 (*si*) | F+ | H3, H5, H7 | Snake | 09:00–10:59 | May |
| E7 | 午 (*wu*) | F– | H4, H6 | Horse | 11:00–12:59 | June |
| E8 | 未 (*wei*) | E– | H6, H4, H2 | Goat | 13:00–14:59 | July |
| E9 | 申 (*shen*) | M+ | H7, H9, H5 | Monkey | 15:00–16:59 | August |
| E10 | 酉 (*you*) | M– | H8 | Chicken | 17:00–18:59 | September |
| E11 | 戌 (*xu*) | E+ | H5, H4, H8 | Dog | 19:00–20:59 | October |
| E12 | 亥 (*hai*) | W+ | H9, H1 | Pig | 21:00–22:59 | November |

For example, as shown in Table 4, the energy of *chou* (E2) is composed of *ji* (H6), *xin* (H8), and *gui* (H10). H8 and H10 are the "hidden stems" of E2. To be more specific, for E2, H6 is the "main energy" (主氣 *zhu qi*), H8 is the "medium energy" (中氣 *zhong qi*), and H10 is the "residual energy" (餘氣 *yu qi*). However, for BaZi analysis, we normally apply only the main energy, as it constitutes the majority of the energy of the branch. The rest only accounts for a small portion. For branch E2, the main energy is that of H6, which is E–. We hence decide that the attribute of E2 is also E–.

The famous twelve animals of the zodiac are also from the 12 branches. For example, the year 2012 is the year of *ren-chen* (H9–E5), the zodiac sign of E5 is a dragon, and hence year 2012 is the year of the dragon. Readers may refer to column 5 of Table 4.

Many readers may have seen fortune-tellers using the twelve signs of the zodiac to tell people's fortune. The zodiac signs were indeed heavily used for fortune-telling before the Tang Dynasty (AD 618–907), but such a practice was deemed inaccurate and thus has been abandoned since Sung Dynasty (AD 960–1279). For modern-day BaZi, zodiacs alone serve little purpose. Nevertheless, there are still many who like to use it to tell their year's fortune. In my opinion, studying one's destiny with only one element, without considering all the others and the interactions among them, is an oversimplification and inaccurate. Many people even use it to decide a couple's compatibility for marriage. I find this ridiculous.

Before the Western 24-hour clock system was adopted, Chinese used the Twelve Earthly Branches to mark the time of day. Each branch represents two hours (as shown in column 6 of Table 4). For example, the hour of *shen* (E9) is from 15:00 to 16:59. It is worth noting that the hour of *zi* (E1) spans two days, from 23:00 of day one to 00:59 of day two. Hence, we normally divide the hour of E1 into "Late E1" (23:00–23:59) and "Early E1" (00:00–00:59).

By combining the Heavenly Stems and Earthly Branches, ancient Chinese created a calendar that cycled every 60 years. One 60-year cycle is called one *jia-zi* (H1-E1). Please refer to Table 5. The year 1984 is the year of H1-E1. The year 1985 is the year of H2-E2, as H2 follows H1 and E2 follows E1. With the same logic, we can derive that the year 1986 is the year of H3-E3, and the years that follow are H4-E4, H5-E5, and so on. The year 1993 is the year of H10-E10, and 1994 will be H1-E11 (*jia-xu),* as the Heavenly Stems already circled back while the Earthly Branches still have two more to go. The year will again cycle back to H1-E1 in 2044, exactly 60 years from 1984.

**Table 5:** The Chinese calendar cycle of sixty

| H1–E1 | H2–E2 | H3–E3 | H4–E4 | H5–E5 | H6–E6 | H7–E7 | H8–E8 | H9–E9 | H10–E10 |
|-------|-------|-------|-------|-------|-------|-------|-------|-------|---------|
| H1–E11 | H2–E12 | H3–E1 | H4–E2 | H5–E3 | H6–E4 | H7–E5 | H8–E6 | H9–E7 | H10–E8 |
| H1–E9 | H2–E10 | H3–E11 | H4–E12 | H5–E1 | H6–E2 | H7–E3 | H8–E4 | H9–E5 | H10–E6 |
| H1–E7 | H2–E8 | H3–E9 | H4–E10 | H5–E11 | H6–E12 | H7–E1 | H8–E2 | H9–E3 | H10–E4 |
| H1–E5 | H2–E6 | H3–E7 | H4–E8 | H5–E9 | H6–E10 | H7–E11 | H8–E12 | H9–E1 | H10–E2 |
| H1–E3 | H2–E4 | H3–E5 | H4–E6 | H5–E7 | H6–E8 | H7–E9 | H8–E10 | H9–E11 | H10–E12 |

What makes this important for BaZi is that such annotation also marks the prevailing energy. For example, the year 2012 is the year of H9-E5 (*ren-chen*). The prevailing energies of the year are that of H9 and E5. The day June 1st, 2012, is year H9-E5, month H2-E6, day H10-E6. We can use the prevailing energies of the day to roughly determine the fortune of a person on that specific day.

# Section 3
# Solar terms of the year

The traditional Chinese calendar was designed for agricultural purposes. Solar terms are specified to mark the seasons to help farmers plan their activities. Contrary to what most people think, the Chinese calendar is not a pure lunar-based calendar, but a mix of both solar and lunar terms. The solar terms, for example, mark the angle of the sun or, in other words, the seasons of the year.

There are 24 solar terms, 12 of which are more important and used in BaZi analysis. The other 12 will not be covered here. The 12 major solar terms are shown in Table 6.

**Table 6:** The twelve major solar terms

| Term | Date |
|---|---|
| Beginning of Spring ( 立春 ) | February 4 |
| Waking of Insects ( 驚蟄 ) | March 5 |
| Pure Brightness ( 清明 ) | April 4 |
| Beginning of Summer ( 立夏 ) | May 5 |
| Grain in Ears ( 芒種 ) | June 5 |
| Slight Heat ( 小暑 ) | July 7 |
| Beginning of Autumn ( 立秋 ) | August 7 |
| White Dew ( 白露 ) | September 7 |
| Cold Dew ( 寒露 ) | October 8 |
| Beginning of Winter ( 立冬 ) | November 7 |
| Great Snow ( 大雪 ) | December 7 |
| Slight Cold ( 小寒 ) | January 5 |

To get the most accurate start and end time of each term, one will need to look up a "perpetual calendar." Since the solar terms are associated with the angle of the sun, which is how the modern day calendar was designed, the dates of each solar term will roughly be the same each year, with only one or two day's variation at most.

Solar terms are needed to build a BaZi chart and to analyze fortune using the chart. As mentioned in the previous section, June 1st, 2012, is year H9-E5, month H2-E6, and day H10-E6. The Beginning of Summer in 2012 is on May 5th, and the order of the term is *yi-si* (H2-E6). This is why we mark that month as the month of *yi-si* (H2-E6).

The same month of a different year always shares the same Earthly Branch (for obvious reasons, as there are 12 branches representing the 12 months), but not necessarily the same Heavenly Stem. For example, the Beginning of Summer term (May) of 2012 is H2-E6, but that term in 2013 is H4-E6. Table 7 lists the period of months based on the Earthly Branches and the solar terms.

**Table 7:** Terms of the months based on the Earthly Branches

| Month | Period |
|-------|--------|
| E3 | Feb 4–Mar 5 |
| E4 | Mar 5–Apr 4 |
| E5 | Apr 4–May 5 |
| E6 | May 5–Jun 5 |
| E7 | Jun 5–Jul 7 |
| E8 | Jul 7–Aug 7 |
| E9 | Aug 7–Sep 7 |
| E10 | Sep 7–Oct 8 |
| E11 | Oct 8–Nov 7 |
| E12 | Nov 7–Dec 7 |
| E1 | Dec 7–Jan 5 |
| E2 | Jan 5–Feb 4 |

# Section 4
# Building a BaZi chart

With what we have learned in the previous sections we can begin building a person's BaZi chart. There are two important elements of a BaZi chart—the Four Pillars (四柱 *si zhu*) and the Grand Fortune (大運 *da yun*). The Four Pillars are the Year Pillar, the Month Pillar, the Day Pillar and the Hour Pillar. To build these pillars, you will need a perpetual calendar (萬年曆 *wan nian li*). If you don't have one, you may also look one up on the Internet. We provide a free website for looking up a person's BaZi chart. Please refer to the instructions at the end of the section.

## The Four Pillars and the Grand Fortune

Before we begin, we will briefly talk about the concept of the Four Pillars and the Grand Fortune.

The Four Pillars, containing eight letters (one Heavenly Stem and one Earthly Branch of each Pillar), can be considered as the basic blueprint of the individual. It tells what the person's character is made of, and it remains the same throughout the life of that person.

The Grand Fortune, on the other hand, shows the general course the person is expected to take throughout his or her entire life. Each Grand Fortune stays with the individual for five years and then switches to the next Grand Fortune.

To help our readers better understand this concept, let's use an analogy. Imagine each person is a car and each a different make and model. The Four Pillars are like the blueprint of the car, and the Grand Fortunes are all the roads it is expected to take throughout its entire life. Every five years it switches from one road to another, and it fairs differently in general. One designed to be a race car may outrun others on the racetrack but may find its speed slowing down when the road of Grand Fortune switches to a mud road. A four-wheeler may fare just the opposite.

## Building a chart

To demonstrate the process of building a chart, we will use an example of a female who was born on June 12, 2012, at 15:30 (hour of E9).

## [Step 1]

First of all, by looking up the perpetual calendar, we find out that June 12, 2012, is year H9-E5, month H3-E7, day H1-E5. The month of H3-E7 corresponded to the solar term of Grain in Ears, which started on June 5 at 14:25 and ended on July 7 at 0:40. We will fill in H9-E5, H3-E7, and H1-E5, respectively, into the pillars of year, month, and day. In each pillar, the upper part is the Heavenly Stem, and the lower part is the Earthly Branch. As the hour of birth is the hour of E9, we will also fill in E9 in the lower part of the Hour Pillar. It will then look something like Figure 2.

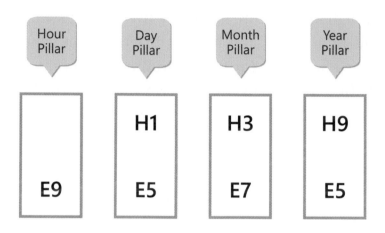

**Figure 2:** Sample BaZi Chart: Step 1

For the sake of simplicity, we will call the Heavenly Stem and the Earthly Branch of the Year Pillar the Year Stem and Year Branch, respectively. With the same logic, we have Month Stem, Month Branch, Day Stem, Day Branch, Hour Stem, and Hour Branch.

## Tip

◆ From my personal experience, the time of birth on one's birth certificate sometimes may be off a little. The actual

Chapter 3
The Basic Knowledge of BaZi

time to be used should be the very moment when the baby's body has contact with the outside air. Since the duties of the doctor and the nurses usually do not stop after the baby is born, the recorded time may be a bit later, depending on the individual situation. If the person does not "fit the profile" of what the chart indicates, you may try to move the Hour Pillar forward by one pillar.

- Always use the local time of the place of birth.

- Pay attention to daylight saving time. If the time of birth is recorded during the period of daylight saving time, please adjust it back to the normal hour.

- In some areas of the world, the time zone is artificially aligned for commercial or political reasons (for example, China is under a single time zone, where in fact it should span across four. Spain uses the same time zone as Germany while it should be two hours apart). In this case, please adjust it back to the appropriate time zone based on the actual geographical latitude of the birthplace.

## [Step 2]

Fill out the Hour Stem based on the Heavenly Stem of the Day Pillar and Earthly Branch of the Hour Pillar. We can do this by looking up Table 8. In our example, the Heavenly Stem of Day Pillar is H1, and the Earthly Branch of the Hour Pillar is E9. We can find that the Hour Stem is H9.

**Table 8:** Obtain the Hour Stem

| | | E1(E) | E2 | E3 | E4 | E5 | E6 | E7 | E8 | E9 | E10 | E11 | E12 | E1(L) |
|---|---|---|---|---|---|---|---|---|---|---|---|---|---|---|
| | | | | | | | **Branch of Hour** | | | | | | | |
| | **H1,H6** | H1 | H2 | H3 | H4 | H5 | H6 | H7 | H8 | H9 | H10 | H1 | H2 | H3 |
| | **H2,H7** | H3 | H4 | H5 | H6 | H7 | H8 | H9 | H10 | H1 | H2 | H3 | H4 | H5 |
| **Stem of Day** | **H3,H8** | H5 | H6 | H7 | H8 | H9 | H10 | H1 | H2 | H3 | H4 | H5 | H6 | H7 |
| | **H4,H9** | H7 | H8 | H9 | H10 | H1 | H2 | H3 | H4 | H5 | H6 | H7 | H8 | H9 |
| | **H5,H10** | H9 | H10 | H1 | H2 | H3 | H4 | H5 | H6 | H7 | H8 | H9 | H10 | H1 |

We then fill H9 into the Hour Stem and get Figure 3.

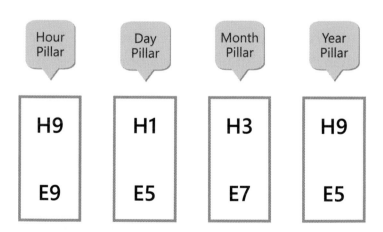

Figure 3: Sample BaZi Chart: Step 2

Now that we have all four pillars complete, we are ready for the next step—the Grand Fortune.

# [Step 3]

We will start calculating the starting point of the Grand Fortune. As the Grand Fortune changes every 10 years, we first need to establish when it first began. To do so, we need to use the person's gender along with his/her yin-yang attribute. We can do so by looking up Table 9.

**Table 9:** Decide the order of the Grand Fortune

| | | Year Stem | | | | |
|---|---|---|---|---|---|---|
| **Order** | Male-yang | H1 | H3 | H5 | H7 | H9 |
| | Female-yin | H2 | H4 | H6 | H8 | H10 |
| **Reverse Order** | Male-yin | H2 | H4 | H6 | H8 | H10 |
| | Female-yan | H1 | H3 | H5 | H7 | H9 |

The way to lay out the Grand Fortune is to traverse through time (either forward or backward) from the time of birth. For yang males and yin females, we lay out the Grand Fortune in a forward order. For yin males and yang females, we do it in reverse order.

The first step is to find the closest solar term to the time of birth. For yang males and yin females, we look for the first solar term AFTER birth. For yin males and yang females, we look for the last solar term before birth. For example, the person is a yang female, so we traverse backward in time and get the nearest solar term before birth to be June 5 at 14:25 (the Grain in Ear). Between the solar term and the time of birth (June 12 at 15:30) are seven days, one hour, and five minutes. We will magnify each three days as one year, and each two hours as 10 days (as mentioned, ancient Chinese divide a day into 12 "Chinese hours," so each Chinese hour is two hours).

With this, we first get seven days into two years and four months (as each three-day period accounts for one year, and seven days equal to 2⅓ years).

We then get one hour and five minutes as 13/12 hours, or 13/24 Chinese hours, which accounts for 130/24 days (5.42 days), with each Chinese hour accounting for 10 days.

We add the two year, four months and the 5.42 days together. We conclude that the Grand Fortune starts roughly two years, four months, and five days after birth. We look up the calendar and find that day to be October 17, 2014, which is nine days after Cold Dew of the year.

Unlike the natural age system adopted by the West, Chinese use a nominal age system, with which a person is one year old right after birth, so we conclude that Grand Fortune starts at the age of three, on the 9th day after Cold Dew.

> **D**o **you know:** the Chinese have been using the nominal age system for a long time, and many still use it today. With the system, a person is already one year old the day he or she was born, and instead of the person's birthday, the age increases at each Chinese New Year. Therefore, a boy born on 2015 will be one year old from the day he was born, and will turn two years old on Chinese New Year in 2016.

## [Step 4]

Now we have the starting point of the Grand Fortune; we will traverse forward/backward from the Month Pillar based on the rule we just laid down, with each month representing 10 years. In our example, we traversed backward. The Month Pillar is H3-E7. The month before it is H2-E6 and the ones before that are H1-E5, H0-E4, H9-E3, H8-E2, H7-E1, H6-E12, H5-E11, H4-E10, and so on. We then mark them as in Figure 4. Since the Grand Fortune starts at age 3 (nominal age), and each pillar rules 10 years, we mark each pillar with age 3, 13, 23, 33, 43, 53, 63, 73, 83.

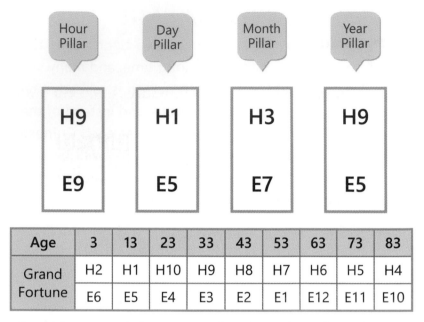

| Age | 3 | 13 | 23 | 33 | 43 | 53 | 63 | 73 | 83 |
|---|---|---|---|---|---|---|---|---|---|
| Grand Fortune | H2 | H1 | H10 | H9 | H8 | H7 | H6 | H5 | H4 |
| | E6 | E5 | E4 | E3 | E2 | E1 | E12 | E11 | E10 |

Grand Fortune switches at Year of H1/H6, 9 days after Cold Dew

**Figure 4:** Example BaZi Chart: Step 3

What this means is that this person starts traversing her Grand Fortune of H2–E6 from the age of 3, the 9th day after Cold Dew. At age 13, the 9th day after Cold Dew, it switches to H1–E5, and so on.

During the ten-year Grand Fortune, the first five years are mainly ruled by the energy of the Heavenly Stem, and the second five years are mainly ruled by the energy of the Earthly Branch. Take our example with the first 10 years of Grand Fortune H2–E6. The first five years the energy of H2 (V-) is strong, and the energy of E6 (F+) is not so obvious. But the second five years (from the age of 8, 9th day after Cold Dew), the energy of E6 becomes dominant.

# Looking up a person's BaZi Chart on a website

Please go to our website. The URL address and QR code are listed below.

**http:**//prof-hwang-fortune-telling.org/en

Figure 5 shows the first page of our website. Please input the year, month, day, and hour of the birth, in order. In this example, we are looking for the BaZi chart of a person who was born on June 12, 2012, at 15:30 (hour of E9).

## Prof. Hwang Fortune Telling

✉ prof.hwang.fortune.telling [at] gmail.com  G·Blog  f Facebook

Today is 2018/11/4, Year of H5-E11, Month of H9-E11, Day of H7-E1.

| 2012 ♦ | Jun ♦ | 12 ♦ | 15 ♦ | 30 ♦ |

**Figure 5:** Our free website for looking up BaZi charts

Once the birth date and time are properly typed in, click the gender of the person (blue for male and red for female). The BaZi chart will show as below in Figure 6.

| BaZi Chart: female, born on June 12, 2012, 15:30 (nominal age: 6) | | | |
|---|---|---|---|
| Es | Self | Cm | Es |
| H9 yang | H1 yang | H3 yang | H9 yang |
| E9 yang | E5 yang | E7 yin | E5 yang |
| Os | Ws | Cs | Ws |

| Grand Fortune | | | | | | | | | |
|---|---|---|---|---|---|---|---|---|---|
| 93 | 83 | 73 | 63 | 53 | 43 | 33 | 23 | 13 | 3 |
| H3 | H4 | H5 | H6 | H7 | H8 | H9 | H10 | H1 | H2 |
| E9 | E10 | E11 | E12 | E1 | E2 | E3 | E4 | E5 | E6 |

Grand Fortune starts roughly 2 year(s), 4 month(s) and 5 day(s) after birth. (2014/10/17 23:44)

Grand Fortune switches at Year of H1/H6, 8 day(s) after Cold Dew.

**Figure 6:** BaZi chart generated by our computer program

The computer-generated BaZi chart on the website includes the most vital information such as the Four Pillars, the Grand Fortune, as well as the timing of the changes of the Grand Fortune. Note that the timing of the changes of the Grand Fortune is slightly different from our hand-calculated result (8 days after Cold Dew from the computer, and 9 days after Cold Dew by hand). This is due to an error in rounding, as computers can calculate up to seconds. In practice, the difference is insignificant and does not affect our analysis.

# Section 5
# Deriving the Ten Spirits from the relative positions of the Five Elements

The Ten Spirits (十神 *shi shen*) is often translated as "The Ten Gods," as if they were the Chinese version of the Twelve Gods of Olympus. This is, in fact, not an appropriate translation, as it has nothing to do with a deity. In Chinese, the word "*shen*" can refer to both god and the spirit of a person. In this context, the latter is the case. Hence we use "Ten Spirits" instead of the commonly used "Ten gods."

The Ten Spirits represent the ten spiritual elements that constitute the unique personality of an individual. In a way, they are like modern-day personality tests, which use a simple matrix to categorize one's personality. For example, the famous Myers-Briggs Type Indicator personality test would categorize one's personality based on the matrix of Extroversion (E)-Introversion (I), Sensing (S)-Intuition (N), Thinking (T)-Feeling (F), Judging (J)-Perceiving (P). The Ten Spirits, in the most basic sense, is similar.

The Ten Spirits are Peers, Creations, Officers, Wealth, and Empowerments, with each a pair of Main and Side (Main Peer, Side Peer, Main Creation, Side Creation, etc.).

It is said that the great scholar of BaZi, Xu Ziping, discovered that, while the eight characters of the Four Pillars all represent the spirit of a person, the Day Stem represents the very center point of the spirit. We call this the Source Spirit (元神 *yuan shen*) or the Host (日主 *ri zhu*). In the context of this book, we will simply refer to it as "Self."

In our example, the Self of a person is H1, with the attribute of V+ (we will represent this in the form of H1 [V+] in the following chapters). The other seven Stems and Branches, based on their attributes, will have production or countering relationships respective to Self. This can be used to derive the Ten Spirits, which can then be used to analyze a person's character, personality, behaviors, and so on. In the following, we will introduce all Ten Spirits.

1. **Those who share the same Element as Self are called "Peers":** Those with the same yin-yang as Self are called Main Peer, and those with different yin-yang are called Side Peer.

   For example, if Self is H1 [V+], then H1 is Main Peer, and H2 [V–] is Side Peer. This is the same for the Earthly Branches. E3 [V+] is Main Peer, and E4 [V–] is Side Peer.

   Take another example: if Self is H5 [E+], then H5 [E+], E5 [E+], E11 [E+] are Main Peers, while H6 [E–], E2 [E–], E8 [E–] are Side Peers.

2. **Those can be produced by Self are called "Creation":** those with the same yin-yang are called Main Creation.

Those with different yin-yang are Side Creations.

Take our example: Self is H1 [V+]. Since Wood produces Fire, then those with the element of Fire are Creations. H3 [F+], E6 [F+] are Main Creations, and H4 [F−] and E7 [F−] are Side Creations.

3. **Those that counter Self are called "Officers"** (think of them as officers who have control and authority over a person): those with "**different**" yin-yang as Self are the Main Officers, and those with the "**same**" yin-yang as Self are Side Officers. Pay attention that the main-side relationship with yin and yang is reversed from here on. Do not be confused. You will understand the reason once you learn the meanings of each Spirit. In our example with H1 [V+] as Self, the Main Officers are H8 [M−] and E10 [M−], while the Side Officers are H7 [M+] and E9 [M+].

4. **Those countered by Self are called "Wealth"** (think of it as anything controlled or possessed by the person): those with "**different**" yin-yang as Self are Main Wealth, and those with the "**same**" yin-yang are Side Wealth. In our example, H6 [E−], E2 [E−], and E8 [E−] are Main Wealth, and H5 [E+], E5 [E+], and E11 [E+] are Side Wealth.

5. **Those that produce Self are called Empowerment:** those with "**different**" yin-yang are Main Empowerment, and those with the "**same**" yin-yang are Side Empowerment. In our example, H10 [W−] and E1 [W−] are Main Empowerment, and H9 [W+] and E12 [W+] are side Empowerment.

Table 10 summarizes the Ten Spirits and their respective relationship to Self.

**Table 10:** Relationship between the Ten Spirits and Self

|  | Abbreviation | Element attribute related to Self | Yin-yang polarity respective to Self | Chinese Name |
|---|---|---|---|---|
| **Main Peer** | Pm | Same | Same | 比肩<br>(*bi jian*) |
| **Side Peer** | Ps | Same | Different | 劫財<br>(*jie cai*) |
| **Main Creation** | Cm | Produced by | Same | 食神<br>(*shi shen*) |
| **Side Creation** | Cs | Produced by | Different | 傷官<br>(*shang guan*) |
| **Main Officer** | Om | Countering | Different | 正官<br>(*zheng guan*) |
| **Side Officer** | Os | Countering | Same | 七殺 / 偏官 (*qi sha*<br>or *pian guan*) |
| **Main Wealth** | Wm | Countered by | Different | 正財<br>(*zheng cai*) |
| **Side Wealth** | Ws | Countered by | Same | 偏財<br>(*pian cai*) |
| **Main Empowerment** | Em | Producing | Different | 正印<br>(*zheng yin*) |
| **Side Empowerment** | Es | Producing | Same | 偏印<br>(*pian yin*) |

Readers who find it difficult to memorize all of these at once can also use Table 11 and Table 12 to look them up.

**Table 11:** Ten Spirits of the Heavenly Stems

| self | | | | | | | | | |
|---|---|---|---|---|---|---|---|---|---|
| **H1** (V+) | **H2** (V-) | **H3** (F+) | **H4** (F-) | **H5** (E+) | **H6** (E-) | **H7** (M+) | **H8** (M-) | **H9** (W+) | **H10** (W-) |
| **H1** Main Peer | Side Peer | Side Empowerment | Main Empowerment | Side Officer | Main Officer | Side Wealth | Main Wealth | Main Creation | Side Creation |
| **H2** Side Peer | Main Peer | Main Empowerment | Side Empowerment | Main Officer | Side Officer | Main Wealth | Side Wealth | Side Creation | Main Creation |
| **H3** Main Creation | Side Creation | Main Peer | Side Peer | Side Empowerment | Main Empowerment | Side Officer | Main Officer | Side Wealth | Main Wealth |
| **H4** Side Creation | Main Creation | Side Peer | Main Peer | Main Empowerment | Side Empowerment | Main Officer | Side Officer | Main Wealth | Side Wealth |
| **H5** Side Wealth | Main Wealth | Main Creation | Side Creation | Main Peer | Side Peer | Side Empowerment | Main Empowerment | Side Officer | Main Officer |
| **H6** Main Wealth | Side Wealth | Side Creation | Main Creation | Side Peer | Main Peer | Main Empowerment | Side Empowerment | Main Officer | Side Officer |
| **H7** Side Officer | Main Officer | Side Wealth | Main Wealth | Main Creation | Side Creation | Main Peer | Side Peer | Side Empowerment | Main Empowerment |
| **H8** Main Officer | Side Officer | Main Wealth | Side Wealth | Side Creation | Main Creation | Side Peer | Main Peer | Main Empowerment | Side Empowerment |
| **H9** Side Empowerment | Main Empowerment | Side Officer | Main Officer | Side Wealth | Main Wealth | Main Creation | Side Creation | Main Peer | Side Peer |
| **H10** Main Empowerment | Side Empowerment | Main Officer | Side Officer | Main Wealth | Side Wealth | Side Creation | Main Creation | Side Peer | Main Peer |

**Table 12:** Ten Spirits of the Earthly Branches

| self | H1 (V+) | H2 (V-) | H3 (F+) | H4 (F-) | H5 (E+) | H6 (E-) | H7 (M+) | H8 (M-) | H9 (W+) | H10 (W-) |
|---|---|---|---|---|---|---|---|---|---|---|
| E3 (V+) | Main Peer | Side Peer | Side Empowerment | Main Empowerment | Side Officer | Main Officer | Side Wealth | Main Wealth | Main Creation | Side Creation |
| E4 (V-) | Side Peer | Main Peer | Main Empowerment | Side Empowerment | Main Officer | Side Officer | Main Wealth | Side Wealth | Side Creation | Main Creation |
| E6 (F+) | Main Creation | Side Creation | Main Peer | Side Peer | Side Empowerment | Main Empowerment | Side Officer | Main Officer | Side Wealth | Main Wealth |
| E7 (F-) | Side Creation | Main Creation | Side Peer | Main Peer | Main Empowerment | Side Empowerment | Main Officer | Side Officer | Main Wealth | Side Wealth |
| E5/E11 (E+) | Side Wealth | Main Wealth | Main Creation | Side Creation | Main Peer | Side Peer | Side Empowerment | Main Empowerment | Side Officer | Main Officer |
| E2/E8 (E-) | Main Wealth | Side Wealth | Side Creation | Main Creation | Side Peer | Main Peer | Main Empowerment | Side Empowerment | Main Officer | Side Officer |
| E9 (M+) | Side Officer | Main Officer | Side Wealth | Main Wealth | Main Creation | Side Creation | Main Peer | Side Peer | Side Empowerment | Main Empowerment |
| E10 (M-) | Main Officer | Side Officer | Main Wealth | Side Wealth | Side Creation | Main Creation | Side Peer | Main Peer | Main Empowerment | Side Empowerment |
| E12 (W+) | Side Empowerment | Main Empowerment | Side Officer | Main Officer | Side Wealth | Main Wealth | Main Creation | Side Creation | Main Peer | Side Peer |
| E1 (W-) | Main Empowerment | Side Empowerment | Main Officer | Side Officer | Main Wealth | Side Wealth | Side Creation | Main Creation | Side Peer | Main Peer |

With our example from the last section, we can mark the Ten Spirits and derive Figure 7.

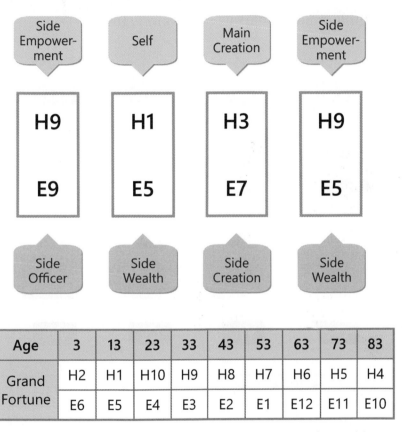

| Age | 3 | 13 | 23 | 33 | 43 | 53 | 63 | 73 | 83 |
|---|---|---|---|---|---|---|---|---|---|
| Grand Fortune | H2 | H1 | H10 | H9 | H8 | H7 | H6 | H5 | H4 |
| | E6 | E5 | E4 | E3 | E2 | E1 | E12 | E11 | E10 |

Grand Fortune switches at Year of H1/H6, nine days after Cold Dew

**Figure 7:** Example of a complete BaZi Chart

The figure can be a bit hard to digest if readers are new to it. To further simplify things we will provide the elements of each Character (Stems and Branches). We will also mark the Ten Spirits with abbreviations, as shown in Table 10. We will get a complete BaZi Chart as shown in Figure 8.

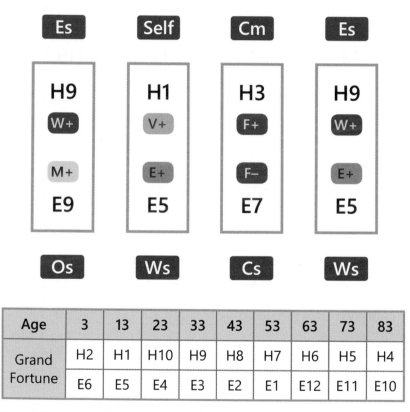

Grand Fortune switches at Year of H1/H6, nine days after Cold Dew

**Figure 8:** Example of a complete BaZi Chart

# Section 6
# The structure (格局 *ge ju*) of a chart

As the chart is built, we will further decide the basic structure of the person. The spirit of the Month Branch decides the Structure. For example, in Figure 8, Self is H1, and the Spirit of the Month Branch is Side Creation. This chart is then called the structure of Side Creation. As it is based on the H1 of Self, we usually call it "Day H1, Month E7, Side Creation Structure" (甲生午月傷官格 *jia sheng wu yue shang guan ge*).

Some schools of fortune-telling simply use self and Structure to judge personality. With the 10 different possible Stems of Self (H1–H10) and the 10 different Spirits, it renders one hundred different combinations. Then they can simply look up the table to decide the personality of the individual. This method, although simple and easy to learn, is not comprehensive, since it does not take into consideration the other six characters along with their interactions.

The foundation of this method is that the strengths of the Five Energies presented in the Four Pillars vary, based on the month of birth. Some schools of BaZi rely on this a lot. Since the element of the month branch is always one of the same as the element of the month of birth, its elemental energy is considered particularly strong. While this is true, the method is still an over-simplification at best. My experience tells me that we should still analyze the whole chart with all its interrelationships among each pillar to get the most accurate information.

# Section 7
# Other important interactions among the Five Elements

In addition to the interaction of production and countering as we have covered up to this point, there are other forms of interactions among the Five Elements. In this section, we will go over the most important ones.

## Yin and Yang

First of all, when we analyze the relationships of production and countering, we need to factor in the yin and yang. The guiding rules are:

1. In the case of countering with the same yin-yang polarity, the effect of countering is strong and severe. For example, H1 [V+] counters H5 [E+]. Since both are with yang polarity, if we only consider the effect of these two, H5 will be seriously countered with its energy entirely suppressed.

2. In the case of countering with yin countering yang, the countering effect is only partial. For example, H10 [W−] counters H3 [F+], H3 is only partially countered. As mentioned before, we may visualize H10 as mist and H3 as wild fire. How can mild moisture as morning mist put out

a wild fire? But the moisture may more or less suppress the strength of the fire.

3. In the case of countering with yang countering ying, we call it "sentimental countering" (剋之有情 *ke zhi you qing*). In this case, the countering effect is also partial. Imagine a powerful warrior facing against a weak lady. How can he bear to apply his full strength against her?

4. In the case of production with the same yin-yang polarity, the production is smooth and complete. For example, H1 [V+] produces H3 [F+], H3 will be greatly enhanced, as a large portion of the energy of H1 is transmitted to H3. This is why we sometimes say H1 "vents" to H3 (洩 *xie*).

5. In the case of production with a different yin-yang polarity, the production is only partial. For example, H2 [V–] produces H3 [F+]. The increase in energy of H3 is only minimal.

# The Clashes (沖 *chong*) of the Earthly Branches

Another important interaction is the Clash. As opposed to Countering, which is one side suppressing the other, Clash is like two elements crashing into each other, resulting in both sides being damaged.

For example, E1 [W-] clashes against E7 [F-]. Based on the rule of countering, E7 will be suppressed. But since E1 and E7 clashes against each other, the energy of E1 will also be damaged. Relatively speaking, E7 still suffers more, as Water counters Fire.

Table 13 lists the six possible clashes.

**Table 13:** The Six Clashes of Earthly Branches

| | |
|---|---|
| **E1–E7** | E7 [F–] suffers more damages than E1 [W–] |
| **E2–E8** | Both E2 [E–] and E8 [E–] are with an Earth attribute. From my experience, this does not cause any serious consequences |
| **E3–E9** | E3 [V+] suffers more damages than E9 [M+] |
| **E4–E10** | E4 [V–] suffers more damages than E10 [M–] |
| **E5–E11** | Both E5 [E+] and E11 [E+] are with an Earth attribute. From my experience, this does not cause any serious consequences |
| **E6–E12** | E6 [F+] suffers more damages than E12 [W+] |

# Coupling and transformation

Here we will discuss the concept of Coupling and Transformation. This is one of the most difficult parts of BaZi analysis, and many schools of BaZi practitioners have different views and approaches, resulting in different interpretations. I had spent years reading through lots of materials from a variety of schools and verified them against many real cases before I finally figured it out with sufficient confidence. Readers are encouraged to read through this section in detail. More examples will be given in Chapters 4 and 5.

The concept of Coupling refers to two Stems or two Branches when put into the same chart and interacting with each other like two magnets. Once two Stems or Branches couple, they lose part of the power to interact with others.

What makes this important is that the effect of coupling may significantly change the result of the analysis. For example, a Stem next to Self that is originally able to support or defend Self from other countering energies may not be able to do so if it is coupled with another. This makes analysis more complicated, especially when we introduce more variables such as annual and monthly flow.

When two Stems or two Branches couple with each other, sometimes one of them may "transform." If there is no transformation, then the two coupled Stems or Branches simply entangle each other, with occasional suppression on one side.

But if one of them "transforms," then things become entirely different. One can think of coupling as two objects combining with each other while still maintaining their attributes and physical properties. But "transform" means it becomes something else—somewhat like a chemical reaction wherein one substance is transformed into another.

Do not feel frustrated if you find this too complicated. Life itself is full of complications. Any model that depicts life with reasonable accuracy cannot itself be overly simple. Just study patiently, step by step, and refer to the basic principle of the Five Elements and yin-yang, and everyone should be able to master it.

Before we go into detailed scenarios of transformation, the following concepts will help readers comprehend better without resorting to memorization.

1. The element that the two coupled Stems/Branches may transform into is called the "Transforming Element" (化神 *hua shen*). The transforming element may not be present on the chart, but we should visualize it as the catalyst between the coupled Stems/Branches. For example, the H1–H6 coupling may transform into Earth (refer to Table 14). Earth is the Transforming Element.

2. In the case of coupling-transformation, we may consider that the coupling effect enhances the force of the Transforming Element. We can then tell easily whether the coupled Stems/Branches gain or lose power with such coupling.

**3.** The conditions required for transformation are quite simple:

🌢 The Stem/Branch needs to sit above/below a Branch/ Stem that either produces the Transforming Element or belongs to the Transforming Element.

🌢 If the Stem and Branch of the same pillar belong to the same Element, then there will be no transformation.

🌢 Self does not transform.

🌢 Month Branch, as mentioned earlier, is a strong branch. It only transforms when the power of transformation is very strong from the Year Branch or the Day Branch.

🌢 Transformation will not happen if the transformed Stem/ Branch is produced by others. This can be explained by the fact that the Stem/Branch is strengthened enough to resist transformation.

Take the example of H1-H6 transformation into Earth, H6 [E-] itself is already with the element of Earth, so there is no need to discuss its transformation. H1 [V+], if sitting on a Branch that belongs to the element of either Earth or Fire (as Fire produces Earth), will transform into the element of Earth. Therefore, in this case, the pillar is H1-E5 [E+], H1-E7 [F-], H1-E11 [E-], and the Wood of H1 will transform into Earth when coupled with H6.

Table 14 lists all five coupling scenarios among the Heavenly Stems. Figure 9 gives a graphic shorthand of six couplings among the Heavenly stems.

**Table 14:** Five coupling-transformation
scenarios among the Heavenly stems

| H1–H6 couple and transform into Earth | H1 [V+] is transformed into Earth if it sits on top of E5, E7, and E11. This enhances the power of Earth but does not necessarily mean that H1 is damaged, since it is already transformed.<br>In the event that H1 is not transformed, the power of H6 will not be seriously damaged. |
|---|---|
| H2–H7 couple and transform into Metal | H7 itself has the attribute of Metal, so there is no need to discuss its transformation. The H2 of pillars of H2–E2, H2–E8, H2–E10 will transform into H8 (M–) with the attribute of Metal if it couples with H7. If there is no transformation, the power of Metal is strong. The energy of H2 will be gravely damaged. |
| H3–H8 couple and transform into Water | The H3 of pillars H3–E1, H3–E5, and H3–E9 transforms into H9 (W+). The H8 of pillar H8–E12 transforms into H10 (W–).<br><br>Pay attention that the attribute of E5 (E+) is neither Metal nor Water, but the hidden branch of E5 contains Water. So this is one exception.<br><br>If H3 is not transformed, the power of Water is strong and will damage the energy of H3. Normally when Fire meets Metal, Fire counters Metal. In this case, however, it damages the energy of Fire of H3. That said, the energy of Metal of H8 is still countered by H3. So this is a lose-lose scenario. Usually events corresponding to suppressed H3 are revealed first, followed by events corresponding to suppressed H8. |
| H4–H9 couple and transform into Wood | The H4 of pillars H4–E4 and H4–E12 transforms into H2 (V–). H9 of H9–E3 transforms into H1 (V+). In the event of no transformation, Wood as the transforming element bridges the two elements (Water produces Wood and Wood produces Fire). As a result, neither side is damaged. The Fire of H4 is not damaged by the Water of H9. |

| H5–H10 couple and transform into Fire | The H5 of H5–E3 and H5–E7 transforms into H3 (F+). The H10 of H10–E4 and H10–E6 transforms into H4 (F–). If there is no transformation, the Fire as transformation element produces Earth, which counters Water. So H10 is damaged. |
| --- | --- |

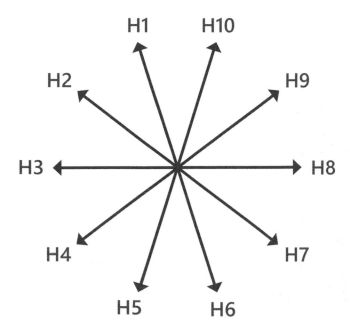

**Figure 9:** A graphical shorthand of the five couplings of Heavenly Stems

For the six coupling-transforming scenarios of Earthly Branches, please refer to Table 14. Figure 10 gives a graphic shorthand of six couplings among the Earthly Branches.

**Table 15:** Six coupling-transformation scenarios
among the Earthly Branches

| | |
|---|---|
| **E1–E2 couple and transform into Earth** | The E1 of H3–E1, H5–E1 transforms into Earth. If E1 is not transformed, E1 is damaged. |
| **E3–E12 couple and transform into Wood** | The E12 of H2–E12 transforms into Wood. If E12 is not transformed, both sides are mutually entangled with no damage on either side. |
| **E4–E11 couple and transform into Fire** | The E4 of H4–E4 transforms into Fire. The E11 of H1–E11 and H3–E11 transforms into Fire. If there is no transformation, E11 gains and E4 loses in this coupling |
| **E5–E10 couple and transform into Metal** | The E5 of H7–E5 transforms into Metal. If E5 is not transformed, it loses in this coupling |
| **E6–E9 couple and transform into Water** | The E6 of H8–E6 and H10–E6 transforms into Water. The E9 of H9–E9 transforms into Water. E6 loses if there is no transformation. |
| **E7–E8 couple and transform into Fire** | The E8 of H2–E8 and H4–E8 transforms into Fire. E8 slightly gains if there is no transformation, but at the same time gets entangled by E7. |

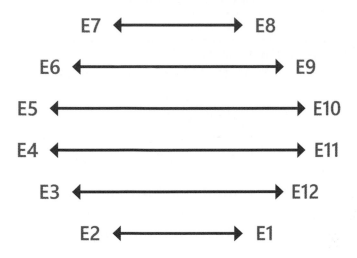

**Figure 10:** Graphic shorthand of the six
couplings of Earthly Branches

Also, the four "hidden coupling" of the Earthly Branches,
although often neglected, should be considered during
analysis. Refer to Table 16.

**Table 16:** The four hidden coupling of the Earthly Branches

| | |
|---|---|
| **E4–E9 hidden couple with Metal** | As the Main Energy of E4 is H2 (V−) and the Main Energy of E9 is H7 (M+), and we learned that H2–H7 couple and transform into Metal, so E4–E9 make hidden coupling of Metal.<br><br>Usually, a hidden couple implies something that happens beneath the surface without being known by others. And since there are other energies of Hidden Stems at play, we do not need to consider transformation. Just think of it as "partially transformed." This applies to all other cases of hidden coupling. |
| **E7–E12 hidden couple with Wood** | Same as above |
| **E3–E2 hidden couple with Earth** | Same as above |
| **E6–E10 hidden couple with Water** | Same as above |

With the above rules, one should pay attention that the transformation does not always occur. Even if it does, it usually is not permanent, as the energies of Grand Fortune, year, and month change over time. Take the example in Figure 11, as H1 sits on top of E11 [E+], the coupling of H1–H6 was supposed to transform H1 [V+] into H5 [E+]. But H1 is produced directly by H9 [W+] next to it, so it remains as it is and does not transform.

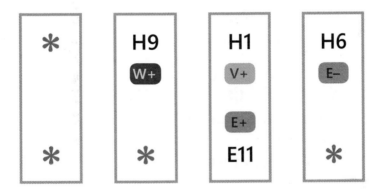

**Figure 11:** Example of a chart

But in the example of Figure 12, H4 [F-] does not produce H1, so we can conclude the H1 is transformed. But during the year of H9, H1 will be produced by the energy of the year, and there may be no transformation during the year. To decide whether the transformation takes place, one needs to consider the strength of H9 of that year and whether there are other interactions in effect.

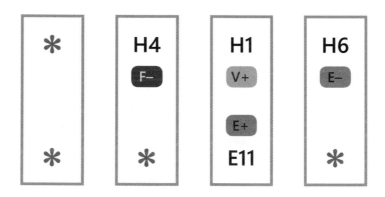

**Figure 12:** Example of a chart

Therefore, it is possible that the status of H1 in Figure 12 changes over time. Sometimes it completely transforms, other times only partially transformed or not transformed at all. It takes a lot of experience to make that judgment. For beginners, simply keep in mind that once coupled, transformed or not, it is trapped from interacting with others. With this in mind, the analysis will not be too far off in most cases.

I have seen many BaZi practitioners not using the principle of coupling-transformation, or simply interpreting it as one of the two Stems/Branches being hurt, without even looking at the Transforming Element. This is such a waste of a valuable piece of information.

Up to this point, we have covered pretty much all the interactions that we will use for analysis. It may require some effort to memorize them in the beginning, but if the readers can practice them with real cases, and better yet, with cases of each type of interaction, then becoming proficient is just a matter of time.

There are other traditional frameworks of BaZi analysis used by many practitioners. These frameworks include Strong Body vs. Weak Body (身強, 身弱 *shen qiang, shen ruo*), the rules of *yong-shen* (用神), and those of *shen sha* (神煞). None of them require detailed analysis of the interaction of the Five Elements. Why?

This is because analyzing the mutual interactions of the Five Elements requires a lot of logical thinking and reasoning. Not every practitioner is able to handle the reasoning process. Therefore, these frameworks were developed so that practitioners can simply memorize the rules and apply them in practice without the need for analysis.

But there are so many possible permutations in BaZi that these rules cannot possibly cover all of them. As a result, they may be accurate on some occasions and inaccurate on others. To cover these "other" occasions, rules of exceptional cases have to be made. In the end, cases of exceptional handling grow exponentially and make it even more difficult to learn. Readers who want to use the foundations of the Five

Element to analyze BaZi must stick with the basic principles of interactions as introduced in this chapter. Once these principles can be applied with ease, all cases can be analyzed naturally.

## Other

The ancient scripts cover many types of interactions. The ones we have covered in this book are the effects of Production and Countering, the Five Couplings of the Heavenly Stems, the Six Couplings of the Earthly Branches, and the Four Hidden Couplings of the Earthly Stems. In my experience, if we can thoroughly take the above interactions into our analysis, it will be quite enough.

Other interactions worth mentioning are the Three Conjoint (三會局 *san hui ju*) and the Three Combination (三合局 *san he ju*) of the Earthly Branches. The Three Conjoint scenarios are:

- ◆ E3, E4, E5 conjoin with Wood (寅卯辰三會木)
- ◆ E6, E7, E8 conjoin with Fire (巳午未三會火)
- ◆ E9, E10, E11 conjoin with Metal (申酉戌三會金)
- ◆ E12, E1, E2 conjoin with Water (亥子丑三會水)

The three-combination scenarios are:

◆ E9, E1, E5 combine Water (申子辰合水局)
◆ E6, E10, E2 combine Metal (巳酉丑合金局)
◆ E3, E7, E11 combine Fire (寅午戌合火局)
◆ E12, E4, E8 combine Water (亥卯未合木局)

The three conjoint and the three combination means the power of the specified element increases. For example, if the Four Pillars already consist of E3 and E4, and the energy of E5 is brought in either by the Grand Fortune, Flow of Year, or Flow of Month (to be covered in Chapter 5), the energy of Wood is considered to be enhanced, since E3, E4, and E5 conjoin with Wood.

But as a matter of fact, E3 and E4 are with the attribute of Wood, and the energy of Wood is strong to begin with. So this does not add a lot of insight. Some of the books use the three conjoint and the three combination to analyze one's marriage. But such an analysis often renders exceptional cases. Hence, we do not intend to cover them here nor recommend this approach.

Other forces of interaction mentioned in the ancient books include destruction (相破), piercing (相穿), and punishing (相刑). If we were to consider all of these interactions, there would be few good days throughout the year. This would render any analysis meaningless. In my opinion, the basic interactions we covered in this chapter are sufficient.

# Chapter 4

## Dissecting the
## Intrinsic Personalities
## with the Four Pillars

# Section 1
# Using the Ten Spirits to
# tell a person's character

With the knowledge of the relationship between the Five Elements and the Ten Spirits derived from it as shown in Chapter 3, we will be able to tell the personality, character of a person, as well as his or her possible academic performance, career preference, potential physical vulnerabilities, and even the lucky colors and directions.

But before that, we have to know the meaning of each Ten Spirit, as well as the luck and incident it represents. This is what this section is about.

When we analyze a person's BaZi, we first analyze the strengths and weaknesses of the Five Elements in the Four Pillars based on the interactions of production, countering, coupling and transformation. The strengths and weaknesses of the Ten Spirits as the result of these interactions will provide us with a lot of information. Details of analyzing strengths of the Elements will be covered in the next section, but as part of the context of this section, we will briefly introduce the basics here. In the context of this section, "produced" or "countered" refers to only those between the two of the same yin-yang (as covered in the previous chapter, strength of production or countering between different yin-yang polarities is a lot weaker).

⬥ A "weak" or "powerless" spirit means either a lack of that spirit in the Four Pillars or that spirit is countered.

⬥ A "strong" spirit means the spirit is sitting inside the Four Pillars, either not being countered by anyone or produced by others.

⬥ An "overly strong" spirit means that the Four Pillars contain either more than two of the same spirits not countered by anyone or one spirit that is produced by two or more other spirits.

With that, we will start introducing the meanings of the Ten Spirits.

## Peers

1. The Spirits of the Peers are those with the same element as Self. These include the Main Peer and the Side Peer. In Chinese, Main Peer literally translates as Peers or "shoulder to shoulder" (比肩 *bi jian*). Side Peer literally translates

as "Rob Wealth" (劫財 *jie cai*), as it counters the Main Wealth. The Spirit of Peers represents self-esteem and self-awareness. It also represents friends, peers, siblings, and the ability to socialize.

2.  On the personality side, persons with a strong spirit of Peers may have the advantage of being self-confident. They can easily form ideas and opinions of their own and are not easily swayed by others. They enjoy making friends and are willing to stake out for them regardless of the cost. They are good at managing social relationships and expanding personal networks. In their minds, once a friend, always a friend.

♦ On the other hand, the disadvantages may show in persons with an overly strong spirit of Peers. They could be very stubborn and opinionated, and they are less concerned about keeping or managing their wealth. This may lead to uncontrolled spending or imprudent investments. Sometime they may also spend too much as they put their own or their friends' needs above money.

♦ Those with a weak spirit of Peers may find themselves not easy to build friendships with others. They get nervous easily and may easily feel unsafe. They usually do not have close relationships with their friends or siblings. Since they lack self-confidence, they could easily be influenced by others.

# Creations

1. The Spirits of Creations are those with the element produced by the element of Self. These include the Main Creation and the Side Creation. In Chinese, the Main Creation is literally translated as "Eating Spirit" (食神 *shi shen*) and Side Creation as "Hurting Officer" (傷官 *shang guan*). As the spirits of Creation are produced by Self, they represent those created by our mind. This refers to our thoughts, intelligence, skills, abilities, reputations, and so on.

2. On the personality side, persons with a strong spirit of Creation usually have high self-esteem and confidence in their ideas. They are likely to be more courageous and willing to take risks. They may be less patient at times. Usually, they are quite articulate and smart and are good at logical reasoning and structural thinking. They are often gifted with one or many talents, such as creativity, imagination, spatial sense, sports, music, literature, dance, and so on.

◖ Many artists, celebrities (actors or singers), athletes, and scientists are strong with the spirits of Creation.

◖ For females, the spirits of Creation also means her child/children. The Main Creation means daughter (as it is with the same yin-yang as Self, which is the mother) and Side Creation means son.

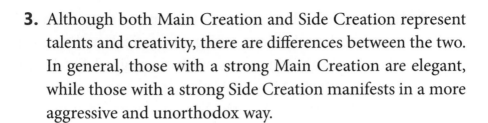 
**3.** Although both Main Creation and Side Creation represent talents and creativity, there are differences between the two. In general, those with a strong Main Creation are elegant, while those with a strong Side Creation manifests in a more aggressive and unorthodox way.

◆ Main Creation

   ✝ Persons with a strong Main Creation may look smart and elegant. They are often talented and good at singing and dancing. They are good speakers and are full of ideas.

   ✝ Persons with overly strong Main Creation may show problems. Although they are full of ideas, they may be all talk, or they are so idealistic that their ideas become unrealistic.

   ✝ Persons who are weak in Main Creation may lack communication skills. They do things the same way and are unable to create new solutions when the situation changes. They tend to be a bit lazy, not willing to take responsibility adapt, or adjust their ways of doing things.

◆ Side Creation

   ✝ Persons with strong Side Creation look smart and aggressive from the outset. They are often revolutionaries and want to innovate or even overthrow tradition. They are good with strategies and prefer to get right to the point when they speak.

✝ However, if Side Creation is too strong, the person will appear to be rebellious, arrogant, cynical, and sarcastic when making comments with no regard for saving face for others. They may also appear to overestimate themselves and make unrealistic goals or insist in doing everything their way. In the end, their attitude may do them a disservice and make them more enemies than friends.

✝ Those who are weak in Side Creation may lack creativity and appear not smart. They could also appear to be passive and lazy, with no ability to think on their feet.

## Wealth

1. The spirits of Wealth represents everything that is owned and controlled by Self. In practice, it represents material wealth, enjoyment, reward, compensation, etc. It also implies change and movement.

2. For males, the spirits of Wealth also represent the wife or girlfriend. Some say that they can also be used to represent the person's father. However my own experience suggests that the accuracy is quite low. Therefore, I do not recommend analyzing it as such.

3. Main Wealth normally implies the normal sources

of income (e.g., salary). Side Wealth may refer to extraordinary or unexpected income (may be large in quantity).

**4.** Regarding personality:

◆ Persons with a strong spirit of Wealth value wealth and put their mind in creating wealth. Males are also popular with females and may win over their hearts easily.

◆ Persons whose spirits of Wealth are too strong may lack perseverance and give up easily. They may be overly interested in material pleasures. In particular, those with overly strong Side Wealth may be prone to gambling addiction or speculative investments.

◆ Males with a weak spirit of Wealth may have more difficulty finding girlfriends or getting married, as they tend to set high standards in their selection of partners, and for those who are in a relationship, they may tend to be less considerate to their other half, either by being picky or over-demanding. Sometimes, they will simply engage in a relationships that is less intimate (e.g., long-distance relationships, or living separately), other times, they may not get married or get married at an older age. They may have little or no desire to pursue material wealth. Some of them lead a simple life with no desire to make money. Others may spend money easily without thinking about saving it.

## Officers

1.  The Spirit of Officers, by its literal meaning, refers to anything that disciplines, controls, or even hurts Self. Officers in a modern-day democratic society may be deemed as public servants. That was not the case in ancient China. To ancient Chinese civilians, government officers had absolute power over them. They could command, control, and punish civilians as they saw fit. Hence, we get the name Officer. For the two Spirits of Officers, the Main Officer usually implies to control or discipline in a civilized manner, while the Side Officer implies a more severe or extreme case that may even cause damage. Hence, ancient Chinese gave the Side Officer (偏官 *pian guan*) another formidable name "The Seven Killings" (七殺 *qi sha*).

2.  The Main Officer typically represents government, rules, position, law, discipline, education and manners, and perfectionism.

3.  The Side Officer (Seven Killings) represents danger, damage, accident, dispute, pressure, suppression, harsh self-discipline, and stress.

4.  For females, Main Officer represents husband. If there is no Main Officer in the Four Pillars, then the Side Officer represents husband instead.

5.  For males, Officers represent children. Main Officer represents daughter, and Side Officer represents son.

**6.** Regarding personalities:

🔹 Persons with a strong spirit of Main Officer are honest and law-abiding. They are careful and meticulous, with a flair for administration and public affairs. They are self-disciplined and appear well behaved.

🔹 Persons with an overly strong spirit of Main Officer may be overly conservative. They tend to be highly indecisive and procrastinate when making major decisions, let alone taking a chance.

🔹 Persons with a strong spirit of Side Officer appear strong-minded and decisive, even a bit fearsome at times. They are goal-oriented and tend to drive themselves hard to achieve their goals.

🔹 Those with an overly strong spirit of Side Officer may be too hard on both themselves and others. They tend to get stressed easily and repress their feelings. They are constantly under pressure and can hardly relax. Some of them may be workaholics or even obsessive-compulsive in some way.

🔹 Persons with a weak spirit of Officers are not good at administration and inefficient in doing things. They do not like to be under authority or discipline, and they may not sit well inside such an environment. As a result, they tend to get into conflicts with their superiors, or get tired of their jobs easily.

## Empowerments

1. The Spirits of Empowerment refer to all things that protect, safeguard, and bring peace of mind to Self, such as parents, faith, religion, Noble Persons (貴人 *gui ren*), employer, law and order, medicine, real estate, power, sense of well-being, sense of security, sense of morality, and sense of dignity.

> **D**id you know: In Chinese, the Spirit of Empowerment is "印 (*yin*)," which literally translated as "seal." The seal is a symbol of empowerment in the ancient Chinese bureaucratic system. All official positions came with a seal, and the Officer assigned to the position would be given the seal under his possession to symbolize his authority and empowerment to perform the duty. Even the emperor carries a seal that represents his imperial authority to rule the nation.

2.

> **D**id you Know: The Noble Person (貴人, *gui ren*) is a commonly used term even in modern day Chinese. A Noble Person does not mean an aristocrat but someone who provides help and support in times of need. For the person being helped, such help may well be precious or even life-changing.

**3.** The Main Empowerment also represents mother.

**4.** Regarding personality:

♦ Persons with a strong spirit of Empowerment usually love to learn. They tend to be kind, easy-going, trustworthy, and they love to help others. They tend to get more support from their seniors, either inside or outside the family, and often find opportunities to be placed in power. Many of them enjoy pursuing spiritual wealth. Those with a strong Main Empowerment are more likely to pursue religion or philosophy, while those with strong Side Empowerment are more likely to pursue metaphysics, mysticism, fortune-telling, and so on.

♦ Persons with an overly strong spirit of Empowerment can be too talkative, passive, or lacking in motivation.

♦ Persons with a weak spirit of Empowerment may feel mentally insecure. As a result, they may get restless in their lives. They tend to move a lot or change jobs easily. They find it hard to keep their promises and often hide their real feelings from others.

Usually, what we see on Heavenly Stems represent what is obvious to others, whether it is personality traits or things that happen. On the other hand, what we see in the Earthly Branches represent things that are more implicit, private, and hidden from others.

When we analyze the strengths of the Ten Spirits of a person, we also need to consider their interactions, such as production, countering, coupling and transformation. This is just like what we introduced in Section 3. See Figure 13.

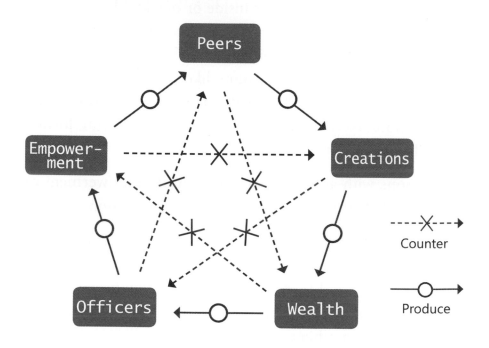

**Figure 13:** The countering and producing of the Ten Spirits

# Section 2
# Analyzing the interactions among the Four Pillars

By analyzing the interactions of the elements in the Four Pillars, we can further tell a person's personality, character, relationship with family and friends, and things that he or she may experience. The basic principles of analysis are:

1. The Heavenly Stems and Earthly Branches should be analyzed as two separate groups. The interactions between adjacent elements should be considered first. Note that the Hour Stem and the Month Stem are considered adjacent (refer to Figure 14).

2. Those manifested from Heavenly Stems are more explicit and known by the public. Those from Earthly Branches are more implicit and private.

3. Rooted spirits and the Spirit of the Month Branch should be considered strong. A "Rooted" spirit means that same spirit is present on both the Heavenly Stems and the Earthly Branches among the Four Pillars.

4. The yin and yang of the Five Elements should be distinguished carefully.

5. Countering, clashes, coupling, and transformation should be analyzed carefully. Pay attention to whether transformation happens with the coupling.

6. The effect of bridging, which will be explained later, should also be considered.

7. In the case wherein transformation does occur, we should also consider other effects that may reverse the transformation.

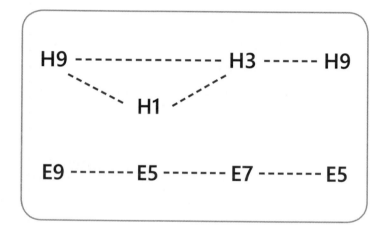

**Note:** Self interacts both with Month Stem and Hour Stem, and we usually plot the Four Stems in a linear format. But when we analyze them we should treat the position of these three as triangular, as shown in this figure.

**Figure 14:** Illustrative example of adjacency among the Four Pillars

Let's practice by examining the Four Pillars in Figure 7. On the Stem side, if we ignore the H1 of Self for a moment, we will see that both the Hour Stem and the Year Stem are H9 (W+), and both directly counter the H3 (F+) on the Month Stem. As H9 represents Side Empowerment and H3 represents Main Creation, this person may suffer serious "Empowerment Countering Creation" (印剋食傷 *yin ke shi shang*). As Creation represents one's talent and ideas, this implies that the person's talent is gravely suppressed. As a result, she may have poor academic performance, and may be fooled easily or make wrong decisions. Luckily both the Month Stem and Month Branch are Creations. The energy of Creation is rooted and quite tough.

Now, as we analyze the countering, we put Self back in the picture. As we have learned, H9 (W+) produces H1 (V+), and H1 produces H3 (F+). So the countering of H9 to H3 is alleviated by H1. This is what we call H1 **"bridging"** the countering. Bridging reduces the effect of countering.

Readers may wonder whether the effect of countering still occurs when bridging is present. Based on my experience, I believe that both effects of countering and bridging will occur. For example, if the bridging energy comes in as the energy of the year, then we may observe that within the year, the effect of countering happens first, and then bridging comes into effect. In our example, the energy of Self bridges the countering. Furthermore, the Grand Fortune between age 13 and 18 is also H1, making the bridging even more effective, strengthening the H3 of Main Creation. Ages 13 to 18 are usually fall between the period of middle and high school. We may reasonably infer that she was able to unleash her talent at school and gain a reputation accordingly.

Since there are two Side Empowerments on the Heavenly Stems, we can also say that the spirit of Side Empowerment is strong. The personality traits of strong Side Empowerment may be seen in this person.

On the Earthly Branch side, The Fire of E7 produces the Earth of E5. Creation produces Wealth. This means that she will be interested in creating wealth. Furthermore, Wealth produces Officer. This means she has the opportunity to be in a managerial or leadership position.

In the following section, I will share the personality traits derived from production or countering among the Ten Spirits. While some are from other earlier books of BaZi and others I discovered through my research, I did verify them all through my practice with real cases. I should also thank my wife (and co-author of this book) for giving me valuable input. We usually practice and discuss cases together. Regarding the personalities of our clients, she is a lot more sensitive and observant than I am, and often she was the one who discovered connections. Readers who may have other insights are also welcomed to drop me an email and discuss.

There is one more thing I would like to remind our English readers. BaZi was originally developed by the ancient Chinese. The judgments on personalities are, inevitably, influenced by or even biased towards ancient Chinese culture and its value system. This may or may not suit the modern Western world. At times, it may even seem politically incorrect. For example, ancient Chinese believed that a good wife should put her husband's needs over her own, and the desired quality of serving in the government is to obey the rules and dictates of superiors. Under such a value system, women who had their own ideas and men who dared to challenge the rules were deemed "out of their place." Such a quality was so undesirable that ancient BaZi masters dubbed it a demeaning name: "Hurting Officer." But in modern society, innovation is a highly sought-after quality, and we see many businesses and political leaders with such a rebellious quality. In this book, we try to remove those biases from the ancient culture. Also, for those statements that may still represent a divide between Eastern and Western cultures, we will mark a [C] in front of the statement. When studying the interaction between the Ten Spirits, readers should focus more on interpreting the internal driving forces than on the superficial behaviors, as the same driving force may manifest different behaviors under different cultures, societies, or even upbringings.

Common traits from the interactions of the Ten Spirits will be described in the next section.

# Cases of Productions

## ✴ Peer produces Creation

### ◟ Main Peer produces Main Creation

† Strong energy focuses on Main Creation. The person has an exceptionally refined intelligence and elegance, a good sense of art and aesthetics, and fine taste when it cause to lifestyle.

† For females, this implies fertility. Such females normally have no problem bearing children, and their children usually do well.

† Those with jobs involving creativity are blessed with ideas and inspirations.

† Those with research jobs have clear minds and can think logically. This helps them with their research work.

† Authors, reporters, or writers are more likely to write high-quality work that earn them a good reputation.

### ◟ Side Peer produces Side Creation

† Strong energy in Side Creation means the person is smart, somewhat proud, with a quality of distinction. They may have unique tastes in art and lifestyle, and may prefer creating new rules than following existing ones.

† For females, it also implies fertility. Children also tend to do well.

+ Those with jobs involving creativity may tend to create avant-garde or innovative works.

+ Those working in the research industry also tend to create or discover unique objects and ideas, including revolutionary theories and new methods and so on.

+ Writers may tend to write critical works, with an edgy or unique way of thinking.

## * Creation produces Wealth

### ◆ Main Creation produces Side Wealth, and Side Creation produces Main Wealth

+ Usually implies that the person can create wealth with his or her skills, talents, or ideas.

+ The person has a desire to create wealth and put his or her mind to it.

+ Outgoing. Enjoys social situations and having fun.

+ For males, this implies popularity with females, and often being a good lover.

## * Wealth produces Officer

### ◆ Main Wealth produces Main Officer

+ Strong energy in the Main Officer implies having the ability and opportunity to assume a managerial or leadership position.

✝ For females, this implies good fortune with men and marriage. Females with such a quality usually play a good supporting role to their husbands.

✝ For males, this implies good fortune with children.

✝ Honest, just, thorough. A law-abiding citizen and a person of honor.

✝ However, over-thoroughness may lead to over-caution and procrastination. Too rigid in following rules may also lead to stubbornness with no room to improvise.

◆ **Side Wealth produces Side Officer**

✝ Strong Side Officer implies a strong ability to execute things and get them done. Active, decisive, determined, goal-oriented. Always accomplishes missions, regardless of the cost.

✝ Constantly demanding perfection, and as a result, always under pressure and finding it difficult to relax.

✝ Sometimes prone to get into trouble (arguments, lawsuits, blackmail, etc.) or accidents.

## ✱ Officer produces Empowerment

◆ **Main Officer produces Main Empowerment**

✝ Possessing the quality to work in large corporation or in the public sector. This implies a good opportunity for promotions and the accumulation of power.

✝ This also implies passive income (for example, rental income, dividends, etc.)

✝ Energy focusing on Main Empowerment suggests that the person is kind, sympathetic, and trustworthy.

✝ Tend to get help and support from "Noble Persons" throughout his or her life. This could be senior members of the family (e.g., heritage), mentors, superiors, or others who offer support. For females, this means a good relationship with the family of the husband.

♦ **Side Officer produces Side Empowerment**

✝ This is also a good sign for a career in a large corporation or the government, with a good opportunity for promotion and empowerment. But in comparison to Main Officer producing Main Empowerment, the energy is fiercer and more violent. This means being busier on the job and perhaps having more pressure.

✝ Energy focusing on Side Empowerment also suggests that the person is kind, sympathetic, and trustworthy, and who receives help from Noble Persons throughout his or her life.

✝ [C] For females, this also suggests a good relationship with the family of the husband and getting along well with parents-in-law.

## ✱ Empowerment produces Peers

♦ **Side Empowerment produces Main Peers, or Main Empowerment produces Side Peers**

✝ This suggests that the person has the fortune of getting a lot of help and support. He may be blessed with family heritage, or receives help from Noble Persons. This also implies that he or she has the opportunity to make passive or stable income.

# Cases of Countering

## ✶ Empowerment counters Creation

### ◆ Side Empowerment counters Main Creation, or Main Empowerment counters Side Creation

✝ Talent and intelligence are suppressed. Lack of ideas and inspiration. Hard to think clearly.

✝ Lack of clear judgment. Easily fooled or tricked.

✝ The person may appear emotionally low and depressed. Sometimes even suffers depression.

✝ For females, this could mean difficulty in giving birth, or even infertility in some serious cases.

## ✶ Creation counters Officer

### ◆ Main Creation counters Side Officer or Side Creation counters Main Officer

✝ The person values individuality and freedom; he or she hates to be chained to any rules, and tends to challenge it.

✝ Easily gets bored with routines, perhaps resulting in frequent job changes. Also prone to disagreements or even conflicts with superiors. It is advised that persons with such a trait be conscious of his or her emotions, use more empathy, spend more time communicating with others, and try to let go of his or her agenda from time to time.

✝ Females might take a stronger or dominating position in the marriage, sometimes leading to friction or conflicts in the relationship.

## ✱ Officer counters Peer

### ◆ Side Officer counters Main Peer

✝ The person tends to set a high standard for himself or herself, and therefore feels insecure or paranoid and constantly under pressure.

✝ The person is prone to getting into trouble or accidents.

✝ Pressure may also come from bosses or superiors.

✝ As the person is stressed, sometimes he or she could be subject to panic attacks, obsessive thoughts, compulsions, or even schizophrenia.

✝ Workaholic. Overworked and stressed easily.

✝ Hard to make friends as others may also sense the stress. It is advised that such a person consciously relax and give themselves a break from time to time. Try to calm down and seek peace of mind through religion, meditation and so on. Sports and routine exercise are also good ways of relieving pressure.

- **Main Officer counters Side Peer**
  - Perfectionist. Dedicated to working wholeheartedly.
  - Too rigid with the rules. Not able to change or improvise.

## ★ Peer counters Wealth

- **Main Peer counters Side Wealth, or Side Peer counters Main Wealth**
  - In the case of males, some demand high standards for their wives or girlfriends. They are prone to be picky or demanding, at times even to the point of being a control freak. Others may have a low chance of meeting the right women, or they may spend little time with them.
  - Do not value wealth. Some of them may either show little desire to make money, or live a simple life with little desire for materialistic things. Others may tend to spend what they make with no discretion. In either case, they tend to have difficulty accumulating wealth.
  - For such persons, it is advised not to engage in gambling or high-risk investments. Conservative investment types such as fixed income, real estate, or systematic investment plans would be better options. Moreover, they may vent their propensity to spend by donating to charity or education.

## ★ Wealth counters Empowerment

### ◊ Side Wealth counters Side Empowerment, or Main Wealth counters Main Empowerment

✝ Mentally restless. Hard to find peace in life. Always on the move, and capricious.

✝ Tends to travel or relocate away from home.

✝ Difficulty keeping promises. They have trouble opening their hearts to others, and they keep their thoughts within. Others may find it hard to guess what they're thinking.

# Section 3
# The Four Pillars and
# the physical health of a person

For most of my clients, health is an important topic of consultation. Figure 15 lists the relationship between the Five Elements and our bodies. For example, if a person shows serious countering with H1 (V+) in his Four Pillars, we may remind them to watch out for problems with the liver, gallbladder, bones, or tendons.

| | | | | |
|---|---|---|---|---|
| H1 | Wood | Gallbladder, bone, (loss of) hair | Rheumatism, fatigue, immune system, nerve system, thyroids | East (Green) |
| H2 | | Liver, hair (grey), tendon | | |
| H3 | Fire | Small intestine (diarrhea), eyes | Brain, tongue, blood pressure | South (Red or purple) |
| H4 | | Heart, blood supply | | |
| H5 | Earth | Stomach, muscle, uterine tumor | Digestive system, belly, lips, breast | Middle (Yellow or brown) |
| H6 | | Spleen, diabetes | | |
| H7 | Metal | Large intestine, hemorrhoids, acne | Nose, sinus, teeth, tonsils | West (White or silver) |
| H8 | | Lung, trachea, skin | | |
| H9 | Water | Bladder | Blood, blood vessel, stroke, gynecological diseases, anemia, lymph nodes, bone marrow, urinary system, reproductive system, prostate gland | North (Black or blue) |
| H10 | | Kidney, ear | | |

**Figure 15:** Common health issues caused by each countered Element.

Although H1 and H2 are listed separately, we should bear in mind that is not always the case. Sometimes symptoms of countered H2 may show in the cases of countered H1, and vice versa. We believe that this is because both have the element of Wood, and yin and yang coexist in our body.

Another thing to keep in mind is that, in the case that H1 is countered, not all listed symptoms of countered H1/H2 will show. Based on my experiences, some clients may show only one of the symptoms, while others show multiple. Sometimes the same client will show different symptoms at different ages. Exact symptoms vary, as each person carries different genes and leads different lifestyles.

The ancient Chinese script of medicine *"Huang Di Nei Jing"* (literally translated as Inner Canon of the Yellow Emperor) revealed the principle that the energies of Wood, Fire, Earth, Metal, and Water correspond to liver, heart, spleen, lung, and kidney. This is based exactly on the same founding principles of BaZi. Even for modern-day Chinese-medicine practitioners, *Huang Di Nei Jing* is a must-read when it comes to studying the relationship between the Five Elements and the human body. Such secret of the interaction between the human body and the Five Elements discovered by ancient Chinese over 2,300 years ago really ought to be regarded as a treasure of Chinese culture.

One of my disciples holds an M.D./PhD from a national university in Taiwan. He was an assistant professor at a medical school and is now a highly reputable Chinese-medicine doctor with his own clinic. While I was teaching him

BaZi, we were able to research large numbers of real clinical cases jointly. Also, throughout my years of BaZi consulting with many of my clients, I was also able to find plenty of cases to confirm the theory and gain further insights. In this section, we will discuss each scenario under which one of the Five Elements is countered.

## Wood is countered

The most commonly seen problems when Wood is countered are related to the liver, gallbladder, tendons, bones, and immune system. There are many liver-related diseases, which we do not intend to list in full. A minor symptom that is frequently observed by clients is proneness to fatigue. Typical problems of the gallbladder include gallstones and acute inflammation. Typical problems with the tendons and bones include frozen shoulder, sprains, and lower back pain.

The problems related to the immune system could be more complicated. Oftentimes, clients are subject to getting colds or the flu easily, but there could also be complications of the skin. Once a professor of a public university sought my consultation. His BaZi chart showed severe Metal countering Wood. I asked him if he had any trouble with his liver, gallbladder, tendons, bones, or immune system, and he was shocked. It turned out that, for years he had been troubled by skin-related problem that could not be treated by a dermatologist. The dermatologist eventually referred him to an immunologist, who discovered that his skin symptoms were, in fact, caused by his immune system.

Other commonly seen problems are those related to the nervous system and thyroids, as well as hair loss, greying hair, rheumatism, and gout. I have another client who is a young lady. She had a hard time figuring out why she tended to fall easily when she walked, and her muscles were slowly losing strength. She consulted many doctors who were not able to pinpoint the cause. She suspected that it had something to do with a major car accident she had years ago, but upon reviewing her BaZi chart, I found an obvious *geng-yi* (H7–H2) coupling, resulting in the Wood of *yi* (H2) to be countered. Furthermore, she had just gone through a five-year grand fortune (luck pillar) of Metal of *geng* (H7). I, therefore, suggested that she get a checkup with a neurologist. A few weeks later, she called to say thank you, as she did consult a neurologist and was diagnosed with a rare disease. Her symptom was caused by a defect in neurons. The doctor hence issued her handicap papers (legal proof of disability). Afterwards, she was able to find jobs that were a lot easier to do, and receive social welfare, which she deserved.

## Fire is countered

Common symptoms caused by Fire being countered are related to the eyes, heart, and small intestine. I have the condition of countered Fire. In the past years, I have been subject to eye-related issues such as macular hemorrhage, floaters, vitreous detachment, and retinal holes. Some of my clients suffer severe myopia or amblyopia.

Problems with the heart can be attributed to many causes. I discovered that many of my female clients with countered Fire have the issue of a prolapsed mitral valve. Those with less severe conditions could observe palpitations, arrhythmia, weak blood supply, and cold hands and feet. The common small intestine issue could be as minor as frequent diarrhea. But I do have a relative who was diagnosed with a rare form of small-intestine cancer. Other physical problems related to suppressed Fire are those related to the brain and tongue.

## Earth is countered

Common problems induced by a countered Earth are those related to the spleen and the stomach. Problems with and diabetes are also common. Many clients with countered Earth have a weak stomach and poor digestive capacity. Many of them are slim and claim that they cannot gain weight regardless of how much they eat. If the client has a direct family member who has diabetes, then the client would usually also have diabetes later in life. I usually advise them to exercise regularly to mitigate the chances of getting diabetes. The youngest client whom I met that had diabetes and a countered Earth BaZi was seven years old.

Other problems include mastitis, breast cancer, uterine fibroids, and issues with myocardium. During the years of 2014 and 2015, the flow of energy on the Heavenly Stem side was H1 (V+) and H2 (V−), and I had two female clients who contracted breast cancer. Luckily, both discovered it at an early stage and were able to recover fully. Women with countered Earth often find trouble secreting breast milk, or get mastitis easily. I also have a few of such cases among my clientele.

## Metal is countered

Cases where Metal is countered may manifest in problems related to the respiratory system, large intestine, and skin. Problems related to the respiratory system could span from the nose, sinus, and trachea, to the lungs. Clients in this category often cough easily and have a sensitive trachea. I have come across some cases in which clients almost died in childhood from pneumonia. There are also cases in which clients were diagnosed with asthma due to long-term coughing.

There are many types of skin-related problems. A common one is severe acne during adolescence. As for the large intestine, constipation or irritated bowels are commonly seen. There are also cases of cancer of the large intestine. Other problems may relate to the teeth and the tonsil. Parkinson's disease is also a related problem.

Most people consider Parkinson's disease a brain disease, but researchers of microbiology at Caltech published an article in the December 2016 issue of *Cell*, indicating that this prevalent degenerative disease is related to microbial changes in the digestive duct. The change in microbial composition in the intestinal duct could facilitate or even cause motor deterioration in the host body, while motor deterioration is the major symptom of Parkinson's disease. Moreover, 75 percent of Parkinson's disease patients have problems with their bowels, most notably constipation. Before the article was published, I had the opportunity to interact with a few clients who had Parkinson's disease. Through analyzing their BaZi, I was convinced that such a disease was related to Fire countering Metal. My observation puzzled me for a long time, as most brain-related diseases are related to countered Fire. The Caltech article helped clear my doubt.

For clients with Parkinson's disease, in addition to recommending them to stick to their medical treatments, I also encourage them to consult a reputable Chinese-medicine doctor for herbal treatments that can vent Fire and reinforce Metal in order to restore the energy balance of the body.

# Water is countered

Countered water may cause problems with the urinary bladder, kidney, blood, and reproductive system. Diseases related to the kidney and urinary bladder are well known. Blood-related problems include leukemia and other bone-marrow-related diseases.

Anyone with BaZi susceptible to countered Water should pay attention to high blood pressure caused by arteriosclerosis, and even stroke. Females should pay attention to gynecological issues, such as menstruation, the uterus, or the ovaries. Problems with the uterus under this category are different from uterine fibroids (which, as mentioned, is caused by countered Earth), and is usually related to a "weak and cold" (Chinese-medicine term) uterus or problems with the endometrium.

For males, countered Water might materialize into problems with the reproductive system. I observed that most males with such countered Water have problems with their prostate when they are past middle age. One of my clients asked me if and when he could have another child. I found that he had strong energies with Officer stars in his BaZi, and there was nothing wrong with the BaZi of his wife, but he had a serious issue with Earth countering Water. I, therefore, asked him if he had had any medical examinations for his reproductive system. He said yes, and he was diagnosed with low sperm activity. However, his wife did conceive and gave birth in 2005. After that, they were not able to have another child in spite of all their efforts.

It was then obvious to me as the annual flow of energy in 2005 on the Earthly branch side was *shen* (E9, M+) and *you* (E10, M−), which helped the bridging of Earth and Water, alleviating the situation.

Ear-related problems are also often related to countered Water. I have one client who is deaf in one ear, and some others with slightly impaired hearing. Moreover, those with countered Water usually have lower-than-average metabolism (weak circulation) and show "wet" physical characteristics (this is a Chinese medicinal term, which usually refers to those with low metabolism). It is recommended that they take regular exercise to facilitate metabolism.

## Others

In reality, many diseases are not caused by one single factor. For example, heart-related problems are often caused by Water countering Fire, such as problems with the valves, murmurs, or a weak heart. But heart-related problems can also be seen in people with Earth countering Water, which exhibits cardiovascular issues (e.g., crown artery), or Wood countering Earth, which exhibits myocardium-related issues.

Another example is that gout patients often have countered Wood. This makes sense, since patients feel joint discomfort, but some show Earth countering Water. In such cases, it is usually diagnosed as low kidney function.

The pupil/doctor whom I mentioned earlier in this chapter once tested me by presenting me with one BaZi chart. He told me that the chart belonged to a patient of his who was receiving kidney dialysis. I examined the chart for a long time and told him that I could see only Metal countering Wood, no matter how I analyzed it, and I could not find a clear indication of countered Water caused by either his General Fortune or the annual flow of energy. I told him that there could be a mistake with the birth date or time associated with this chart. To my surprise, he told me that this patient indeed started with liver problems. In the process of trying to improve the condition of his liver, the patient took too many unprescribed and unapproved medications, which not only did not cure his liver but damaged his kidney instead.

Usually, if we discover any one of the five elements to be seriously countered, we would remind the person to take extra care with the corresponding body parts or organs, and to get regular and thorough health check-ups. We may also suggest that they seek help from Chinese medicine to balance the energy of the five elements inside their body.

Up to this point, readers should have realized that the art of BaZi based on the Five Elements and its variations can reveal much information. This book only covers a portion of it. For those who wish to further master this art, the best way to start is to lay out the BaZi charts of family members and close friends, then try to analyze them using the methods covered in this book. Once one can match the analysis against most of the cases, he would have the basic level of competence, which may have surpassed many "professionals" in the market.

In addition to the Four Pillars, the Grand Fortune, Year Flow, and Month Flow can also affect our analysis of a person. For example, many BaZi practitioners would judge that a male with no Wealth in his Four Pillars will find it hard to enter into a marriage. In reality, however, we can easily find exceptions. This is an example of a failure to take Grand Fortune, Year Flow, and Month Flow into consideration. In reality, even if a male does not have Wealth in his Four Pillars, he may still have a happy marriage if Wealth comes in at the right time through the Grand Fortune or Year Flow, and creates a favorable energy flow with his other elements in the Four Pillars.

At this point, let's practice incorporating the Grand Fortune into our analysis. The way to do this is to add one "extra pillar" of Grand Fortune on the side of the Four Pillars. In the next section, we will work on a few case studies to illustrate.

## Section 4
## Case Examples

With all we have learned so far, let's go over a few real cases with my analysis.

# Example A (Male)

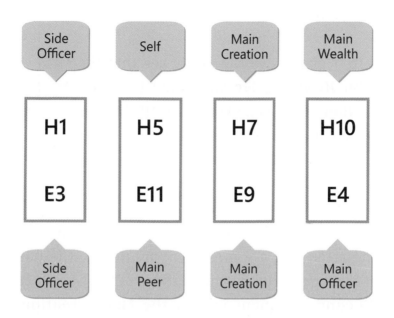

**Figure 16:** BaZi Chart for Example A

| Age | 6 | 16 | 26 | 36 | 46 | 56 | 66 | 76 | 86 |
|---|---|---|---|---|---|---|---|---|---|
| Grand Fortune | H6 | H5 | H4 | H3 | H2 | H1 | H10 | H9 | H8 |
| | E8 | E7 | E6 | E5 | E4 | E3 | E2 | E1 | E12 |

The figure above shows the BaZi chart of a male client. The text in Figure 16 are comments I provided to the client based on my analysis. Let's go over it one by one and not forget the basic rules: to read Heavenly Stems and Earthly Branches separately, and to pay attention to the cases of rooting where the same spirit shows both in the Heavenly Stem and Earthly Branch.

Upon first glance, we can easily see that the Main Creation is undoubtedly strong. For starters, it is rooted. Moreover, the Main Creation of H7 is produced by H5 on the Heavenly Stem side, and the Main Creation of E9 on the Earthly Branch side is not only the Month Branch but also further produced by E11. Unquestionably, this chart belongs to someone with a very strong spirit of Main Creation.

It turned out that the client of this chart is a famous Bonsai gardening artist and a professional art dealer. His talent and tastes in fine arts certainly match the profile of his BaZi chart.

The second comment is that the Main Creation of H7 produces Main Wealth of H10. Such production would have been a lot stronger if it were H9 instead of H10.

The third comment derived is that the Main Creation counters Side Officer on both the Heavenly Stem and the Earthly Branch. By default, the Side Officers are countered. However, when the external energy of H2 comes in (from Grand Fortune, Year Flow, or Month Flow), H2–H7 coupling occurs. Although H2 is the side that gets hurt, the energy of H7 is also tied up and not able to counter the Side Officer of H1. As a result, the energy of H1 will suddenly emerge. Also, the energy of H9 can bridge the countering of H7–H1 and, as a result, enhance the energy of H1.

The fourth comment is based on the fact that E4 is sitting peacefully without being produced or countered. Note that the coupling of E4–E11 does not harm E4.

The 5th and 9th comments regard the luck of the person under the influence of different Grand Fortunes, Year Flows, and Month Flows. Readers may revisit this part after finishing reading Chapter 5, Section 3.

The 10th comment is made as the chart shows severe Metal countering Wood. Hence, we remind the person to pay attention to related health issues and maintain a proper lifestyle as such. As for lucky colors, red and purple may help counter the violence of the rooted Side Officer, while blue and black may bridge the Main Creation countering Side Officer.

**Mr. X is with Day H5, Month E9, and a Main Creation Structure. This chart belongs to one of great talent, intelligence, and creativity.**

1. H5 produces H7 on the Heavenly Stems, and E11 produces E9 on the Earthly Branches. The energies not only concentrate on Main Creation but is also rooted. This suggests that the person has great talent and the characteristics of an artist. It also suggests a person with good communication skills and taste for food. It is best to pursue careers that require communications skills, creativity, or intellectual capacity.

2. Main Creation of H7 produces Main Wealth. This implies the person is capable of creating wealth with his talents. This part is extremely important, as many people with the BaZi structure of an artist lack Wealth. This chart, on the other hand, suggests that the person can not only apply his talents to creating wealth but also be a caring husband or boyfriend to his other half.

3. Both H7 countering H1 and E9 countering E3 show severe Main Creation countering Side Officer. This suggests that the person can be highly opinionated. He is likely to challenge the system and authority if he finds them unreasonable. As a result, he prefers innovation and creation and, from time to time, may feel bored with his job. It is advised that the person pay attention and use more understanding and empathy in the workplace. It will be good to communicate more with his colleagues and superiors, and to avoid being too opinionated.

4. Main Officer of E4 sits uninterrupted. Main Officer suggests that the person has a noble character and is honest and respectable. He is meticulous and has good management skills.

5. During the Periods (Grand Fortune, Year Flow, or Month Flow) of Fire (H3, H4, E6, E7)—the energy of Empowerment arrives. Empowerment represents Noble Persons, or Seniors, and implies support and assistance from such persons. Although the energy of Empowerment may suppress the talent of Main Creation, generally speaking the energy of Empowerment is a blessing, and may also bring wealth.

6. The Periods (Grand Fortune, Year Flow, or Month Flow) of H8, H9, and E12 suggests Main Creation producing Main Wealth. The person has good opportunity to create wealth with his talents.

7. The Periods (Grand Fortune, Year Flow, or Month Flow) of H9 and E12 are related to accidents, stress, disputes, and diseases. During these periods, try to exercise more and reach out for help when needed. Wearing red clothing/ accessories and donating blood can also help alleviate the energy.

8. The Periods (Grand Fortune, Year Flow, or Month Flow) of H5, H7, E5, E9, E10, and E11 suggest Creation countering Officer. The person may easily challenge authority or get tired of his job, as he tends to be more opinionated. It is suggested that the person use more self-awareness during the period and pay attention to the interactions with his peers and superiors. It is advised that he does not insist on his own opinions too much or provoke arguments.

9. The Periods (Grand Fortune, Year Flow, or Month Flow) of H6 are the periods of Self countering Wealth. It is not advised to make any aggressive or risky investments during these periods, as the person is prone to losing or spending money. Conservative investments, healthy spending, or donations to charities may be conducted with caution to vent the energy of Self countering Wealth. At the same time, pay attention to getting along with your wife or girlfriend. Be more sensitive and understanding.

## Example B (Female)

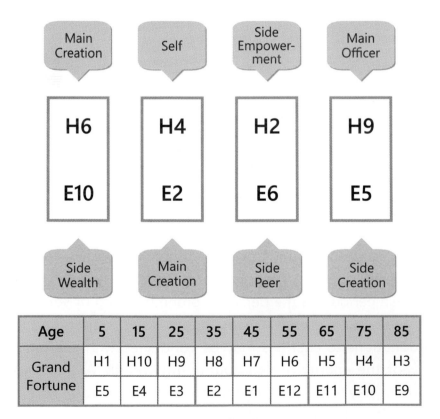

**Figure 17:** BaZi Chart of Example B

| Age | 5 | 15 | 25 | 35 | 45 | 55 | 65 | 75 | 85 |
|---|---|---|---|---|---|---|---|---|---|
| Grand Fortune | H1 | H10 | H9 | H8 | H7 | H6 | H5 | H4 | H3 |
| | E5 | E4 | E3 | E2 | E1 | E12 | E11 | E10 | E9 |

The following are my comments on the BaZi chart in Figure 17. The person is the daughter of my friend, born at a time picked by myself. Over the years, I have been able to observe her growth and development first-hand. As the entire chart shows production with no major countering, the person is healthy and has no physical problems. She has a stable personality and is liked by all.

My first comment is derived from H9 producing H2. The second comment addresses the three obvious Spirits of Creation in the Four Pillars. The third comment about females with Main Officer having a fair appearance and educated behavior is based on my own experience of reading the charts of many female clients. The fourth comment should be fairly easy for our readers by now. The 5th to 9th comments are reminders under different periods of Grand Fortune, Year Flow, and Month Flow. Readers may revisit them after studying Chapter 5, Section 3. As this chart shows no major countering, I did not offer any advice on physical condition or lucky colors.

This woman has Day H4, Month E6, Side Peer Structure. The energy flows smoothly in production in the entire chart. This is an exceptionally good chart.

1. H9 producing H2 creates the momentum of Officer producing Empowerment. This implies not only gaining power in the workplace, but also getting along well with husbands, in-laws, and other senior family members. The strong energy feeding to Spirits of Empowerment suggests that the person has many opportunities to receive help from Noble Persons or senior members of the family or workplace throughout her life.

2. H2 produces H4, which then produces H6. Strong energy focuses on Main Creation. Also, the Main Creation of E2 sits uninterrupted. Energy of Main Creation is very strong in this chart. On top of this, the E6 produces Side Creation of E5. Side Creation is also strong. With the energy of both Main and Side Creations, the person should be highly intelligent and gifted, with an outstanding and elegant quality. She should be able to study art, music, or other performance arts with ease and has great potential to master them. As Side Creation also represents the character of innovation, the person should also have what it takes to create and innovate—a rare combination of both qualities.

3. The Main Officer of H9 suggests that the person is well behaved in class. It also suggests that she has a fair appearance and good conduct.

4. E2 producing E10 smoothly suggests strong Creation Producing Wealth. The person can create wealth with her talents, whether by running her own business or working in a company. As the person is likely to be gifted, it is advised that she chooses a career that can fully utilize her talents (for example, ones that requires communication, intellectual reasoning, creativity, design, planning). She would be able to exhibit outstanding performance in these areas.

5. In the periods (Grand Fortune, Year Flow, or Month Flow) of H1 or H10, the momentum of Officer Producing Empowerment rises. This suggests good opportunities to make passive income, get promotions and gain power, obtain degrees or certificates, acquire real estate, or get help from Noble Persons.

6. In the periods (Grand Fortune, Year Flow, or Month Flow) of H8, E2, E8, E9, and E10, the momentum of Creation Producing Wealth is even stronger. The person will have a better opportunity to create wealth with her talents.

7. In the periods (Grand Fortune, Year Flow, or Month Flow) of H4, H6, E6, E7, E2, E8, E5, and E11 are periods of ideas, muses, creation, and fame. The person should use the time to brainstorm more, as she may find it easier to get ideas and inspirations.

# Example C (Female)

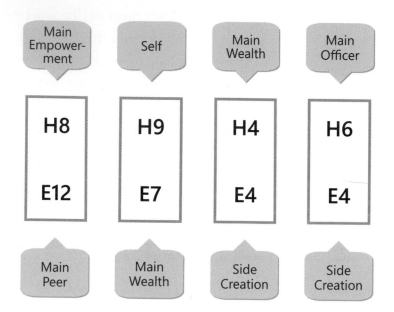

| Age | 2 | 12 | 22 | 32 | 42 | 52 | 62 | 72 | 82 |
|---|---|---|---|---|---|---|---|---|---|
| Grand Fortune | H5 | H6 | H7 | H8 | H9 | H10 | H1 | H2 | H3 |
| | E5 | E6 | E7 | E8 | E9 | E10 | E11 | E12 | E1 |

**Figure 18:** BaZi Chart for Example C

The following is my analysis of the female with BaZi chart shown in Figure 18. This is an exceptionally good one. A child with such a smooth BaZi is likely to be blessed with a healthy and stable personality and is expected to grow up without trouble. In this chart, there is a transformation from the H4–H9 coupling. The coupled H4 transforms into H2, which is Side Creation in this case. Note that Transformed Side Creation, unlike an actual one, does not counter the Main Officer. It merely shows its characteristics. As such, the Officer Producing Empowerment remains intact on the Heavenly Stem side. This person, who is a high-school student, indeed has been assuming leadership roles at school since childhood and has shown great managerial skills. Her teachers like her and often empowered her with significant roles in major school events. Her personality also makes her able to easily find help along the way.

On the Earthly Branch side, the Side Creation creating Main Wealth is also apparent. In school, she ran fund-raising activities for her club. She was always able to get sponsorship and reach the target. I believe such talent will also shine in her future career.

As before, the fifth to the eighth comments is how this chart may be influenced by different Grand Fortune, Year Flow, and Month Flow.

This chart, the "Day H9, Month E4, Side Creation Structure" is an exceptionally good chart. The energies flow with productions throughout. This is a chart of someone with great intelligence and boldness to create and innovate. It also suggests great talent in people management, with an opportunity to gain power at the workplace, as well as creating wealth with one's own skills.

1. The coupling of H4–H9 transforms the Fire of H4 into the Wood of H2, which is the Side Officer. On top of that, the two Side Creations of E4 sit uninterrupted. The Spirit of Side Creation is strong. As Side Creation represents intelligence and talent, the person should be smart and logical, with the talent for the art, music, or sports. The person should also possess a refined task when it comes to food and lifestyle. She is eloquent and possesses the boldness to innovate or even to revolutionize things. she is advised to fully utilize such gifts and pursue a career along the above directions.

2. The H6 producing H8 is the highlight of this chart. This Main Officer Producing Main Empowerment signifies that the person can do well in corporate or governmental sectors and will have the good fortune of obtaining promotions gaining power. The Main Officer also represents good behavior. The person is likely to be pleasant in appearance and temperament, as well as being well-educated in manners. The energy of Empowerment implies the person is kind-hearted and trustworthy. It also implies that the person has help from Noble Persons throughout her life. She may also show interest in studying religions or the art of destiny (BaZi, astrology, etc.)

3. Another highlight is the two E4 producing E7. The Side Creation Producing Main Wealth is strong. This typically implied the ability to make money with her skills and talents.

4. The H9 of Self and E12 of Main Peer are not countered. The Spirit of Main Peer is strong. This implies the person can form her thoughts and opinions without outside influence. This also means high intelligence with the ability to reflect within.

5. The periods (Grand Fortune, Year Flow, or Month Flow) of H2, H4, H6, and H8 are the period of strong Officer Producing Empowerment. There will be opportunities for making passive income, getting promotions and degrees, acquiring real estates, and receiving help from Noble Persons.

6. For the periods (Grand Fortune, Year Flow, or Month Flow) of H2, E4, and E7 are strong periods of Creation Producing Wealth. The person will be able to create wealth with her talents and ideas.

7. For the periods (Grand Fortune, Year Flow or Month Flow) of H5, E5, and E11—the person is advised to pay attention to accidents, stress, backstabbers, disputes, litigations, and even diseases. During such periods the person is advised to exercise more and reach out for help when needed. Wearing white or silver clothes and accessories or donating blood may help alleviate the energy. In addition, the person should also pay attention to diseases related to bladder, kidney, blood, urinal system and so on.

8. The periods (Grand Fortune, Year Flow, or Month Flow) of H9 and H10 suggest losing or spending money. During such periods it is advised not to make any risky or speculative investments. Instead, conservative investments such as fixed-income investments, healthy spending (on education, family trips, etc.), and even donations to charity may help to alleviate the energy.

## Example D (Male)

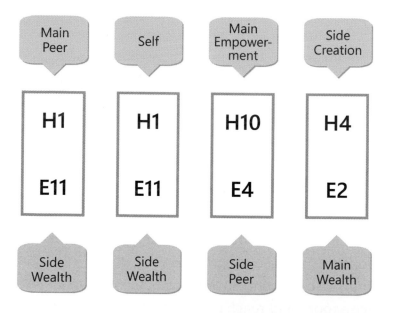

| Age | 10 | 20 | 30 | 40 | 50 | 60 | 70 | 80 | 90 |
|---|---|---|---|---|---|---|---|---|---|
| Grand Fortune | H9 | H8 | H7 | H6 | H5 | H4 | H3 | H2 | H1 |
| | E3 | E2 | E1 | E12 | E11 | E10 | E9 | E8 | E7 |

**Figure 19:** BaZi Chart for Example D

Below is the analysis of the BaZi chart for Figure 19. This is an interesting case. Upon first look it is easy to spot the Main Empowerment of H10 countering the Side Creation of H4, and Side Peer of E4 countering the Main Wealth of E2. But upon further study, we find the two H1 producing H4. Although it's a yang-yin production, two yang wood can still inject a significant amount of power to help it from being completely wiped out by H10. In addition, the two E11 couple the E4, tying up most of its energies from countering E2. The two weak points of the chart therefore are mitigated. In addition, the two E11 are transformed into Main Creation of E6 through the coupling. As a result, the person shows both characters of Main Creation and Side Creation.

In real life, this young man is an avid sports lover who is especially enthusiastic about cycling. He has challenged some extreme routes throughout Taiwan, riding hundreds of miles a day or into steep mountains. Since he has no Spirit of Officers in his chart, he is a bit short on self-discipline and did not manage his schoolwork well. As a result, he did not obtain his high-school diploma. On the other hand, he was extremely dedicated and hard-working in matters that interested him, to the point of not eating or sleeping. Throughout his high-school years, he did not care about studying but was crazy about movies. He spent his time watching and studying movies, and even tried to write his own scripts. Eventually, he was admitted to college with a major in cinematic art.

This is a person with "Day H1, Month E4, Side Peer Structure." The chart shows that the person is blessed with the help of Noble Persons.

1. The Main Empowerment of H10 reveals the person as kind-hearted and trustworthy. As Main Empowerment also signifies Noble Persons and seniors, the person is likely to receive help from them, or be blessed with inheritance. It also suggests that the person may be interested in religion or the art of destiny (BaZi, astrology, etc.) at some point in his life.

2. Despite H10 countering H4, the two H1 injects energy into H4. So the Side Creation of H4 still has half of its strength left. Also, the two E11 transform into Main Creation of E6. Therefore, the person carries the characteristics of both Main and Side Creations. The Spirit of Creation is about intelligence, talent, and art. This suggests the person is smart, with a good sense of logic and creativity and may succeed in studying art, performance, or sports. Also, as Side Creation signifies innovation, the person may choose a career related to communications, research, creativity, design, or planning.

3. Both Side Wealth of E11 and Main Wealth of E2 sit uninterrupted. The person should have good fortune with wealth.

4. The two H1's of Main Peer sit uninterrupted, along with the E4 of Side Peer. The Spirit of Peer is strong. The person is highly self-aware and can form his own ideas without being easily influenced by others.

5. The periods (Grand Fortune, Year Flow, or Month Flow) of H8 signify Officer Producing Empowerment. During these periods, it is possible to make passive income, get promotions and degrees, acquire real estate, or get help from Noble persons.

6. The periods (Grand Fortune, Year Flow, or Month Flow) of E6 and E7 signify Creation Producing Wealth with good opportunities to create wealth with his talents and skills.

7. The periods (Grand Fortune, Year Flow, or Month Flow) of H7 and E9 suggest the need to pay attention to accidents, stress, disputes, arguments at the workplace, and diseases. During these periods, the person is advised to exercise and reach out for help from seniors. Also, wearing blue or black clothes or donating blood can help mitigate the risk.

8. In the Periods (Grand Fortune, Year Flow, or Month Flow) of H10 and H8, the Main Empowerment Countering Side Creation is enhanced. The person may experience the following: difficulty making money, lethargy, suppressed talent, depression, misjudgement or even being cheated. The person is advised to seek assistance and counsel from friends and family more often, and engage in more outdoor activities to help mitigate depression.

9. The Periods (Grand Fortune, Year Flow or Month Flow) of E3, E4, and E1—it is advised not to engage in aggressive or risky investments to avoid losing money. Conservative investments, healthy spending or donation to charities may help mitigate the propensity to spend during such period. Also, it is good to pay attention to the relationship with wife or girlfriend and try to be sensitive and understanding.

10. For physical health, pay attention to Fire (small intestine, eyes, heart, brain, tongue) and Earth (stomach, digestion, muscle, spleen, diabetes) related issues.

11. Lucky colors—Green (intelligence); Red and purple (wealth).

## Example E (Female)

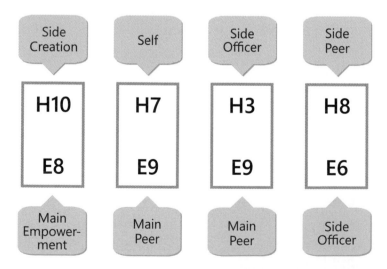

**Figure 20:** BaZi Chart for Example E

Figure 20 is a rare case. The H3–H8 coupling makes H3 transform into H9 of Main Creation. Also, the E6–E9 coupling also makes E6 transform into H12 of Main Creation. As both H3 and E6 are transformed, they are not damaged by the countering-coupling. In fact, through my observation of the person over the years, there has been no sign that shows H3 and E6 being damaged. On the contrary, she is quite gifted in writing, painting, and calligraphy. This matches the analysis that both Side Officers transform into Main Creations.

But it should be noted that when there is the external energy of H1 or H2, the Side Officer of H3 reverts back. As a result, accidents, pressure, or sickness is possible. The person often suffers from chronic coughing during the months of H1. Also, she once fell from a bicycle during this period and fell again before the wound fully healed, which left a quite visible scar as a result.

In the next chapter, we will begin discussing a person's fate under the influence of Grand Fortune, Year Flow, and Month Flow. Before entering this chapter, readers should because proficient with what we have covered so far. Try to get the birth date and time of 20 people whom you know well. Study their BaZi chart carefully and compare it against their personalities, careers, lifestyles, and behaviors. If you find a major discrepancy in any of the cases you collect, try to examine the time of birth (i.e., whether it is offset by Daylight Saving time, the longitudinal location, etc.). Once all the cases can be analyzed, readers should be ready to proceed to the next chapter.

# Chapter 5

# The Science of BaZi Analysis: Grand Fortune, Year Flow, and Month Flow

In the previous chapter, we discussed how to tell a person's character through his or her Four Pillars, as well as an individual's fortune under a given Grand Fortune.

In reality, our fortune changes along with the energy of the nature that surrounds us. The energy changes along with the year and the season. Hence it is different each month. In fact, the energy changes even day by day. But generally speaking, the energies of Grand Fortune, Year Flow, and Month Flow are more impactful, so we usually consider those. Hence, to analyze the overall fortune of a given year, we need to consider the Four Pillars, Grand Fortune, and Year Flow. To analyze the fortune of a given month, we need to consider the Four Pillars, Grand Fortune, Year Flow, and Month Flow. To analyze the fortune of a given day, we need to consider the Four Pillars, Grand Fortune, Year Flow, Month Flow, and Day Flow.

From my own experience, analyzing the fortune of a year with only the Four Pillars, Grand Fortune, and Year Flow might not be enough. This is because most of the people who seek help have certain matters that concern them, and they usually want to know the start and end point of these matters up to the month.

For example, I have a client who is going through a mid-life crisis. He lost his job in a reputable high-tech company and is hoping to start his own business. If we want to help him with our BaZi analysis, the first thing we have to do is to establish his confidence in our analysis. In my experience, the best way to achieve this is to directly point out the cause of the matters that concern him and the months when these matters are in effect. Once he is convinced, he is more willing to open up for consultation. In this case, the matter that concerns him is losing his job. So when he first reached out to me in an email, I briefly replied to him and pointed out his trouble. Here is a part of my reply:

"From the end of 2007 to June 2009, there was an energy of Wealth on Earthly Branch. It bridged the Main Creation Countering Side Officer and made things smooth at the workplace. But once this energy of Wealth ended in June 2009, Main Creation Countering Side Officer started to be in effect. The situation could have been serious in August and September. During these two months, you might have thought of quitting your job. On March 2010 the force of Main Creation was enhanced. It was likely that you got into some form of conflict or dispute with your company or superiors, and left the company as a result."

The gentleman immediately replied and asked to meet me in person. A few days later we had a thorough face-to-face discussion, in which I gave him advice on facing his mid-life crisis and starting his own business. At the end of our discussion, he felt a lot happier and more confident facing his future.

The gentleman told me that, in my email response I clearly specified the months when the events occurred, which were

all quite accurate. He, therefore, decided to seek my advice further. This example suggests that, to properly help others or practice professionally using BaZi, one has to be at least able to analyze up to Month Flow with ease. Without such accuracy, it may not be helpful to the clients.


# Section 1
# The energy of Year Flow

In addition to the Grand Fortune, which was introduced in Section 4 of Chapter 3, here we will introduce the Year Flow. People have different opinions about the start and end point of the Year Flow. Some say it starts on January 1st of each year and ends on December 31; others say it starts on the first day of Spring each year and ends the day before the next first day of Spring. Others believe that the first half of the year is dominated by the energy of the Heavenly Stem, and the second half dominated by the energy of the Earthly Branch.

In fact, the energies of the Heavenly Stem and Earthly Branch of a Year Flow run separately. Each starts from the month when the same energy appears, either during that year or the previous year. It then keeps going until the month when the same energy is countered. With this principle, the energy of Year Flow may be in effect throughout a single continuous period or split into two periods.

Please refer to Figures 21 and 22.

| Month | Feb | Mar | Apr | May | Jun | Jul | Aug | Sep | Oct | Nov | Dec | Jan |
|---|---|---|---|---|---|---|---|---|---|---|---|---|
| | E3 | E4 | E5 | E6 | E7 | E8 | E9 | E10 | E11 | E12 | E1 | E2 |
| Start date | 2/4 | 3/5 | 4/5 | 5/5 | 6/5 | 7/7 | 8/8 | 9/8 | 10/8 | 11/7 | 12/7 | 1/5 |
| H1 | H1/H10 | H1/H10 | H1/H10 | H1/H10 | H1 | | | | H1 | H1/H2 | H1/H2 | H1/H2 |
| H2 | H1/H2 | H1/H2 | H1/H2 | H2 | | | | H2 | H2/H3 | H2/H3 | H2/H3 | H2/H3 |
| H3 | H2/H3 | H2/H3 | H3 | | | | H3 | H3 | H3 | H3 | H3 | H3 |
| H4 | H3 | | | | | H4 | H4 | H4 | H4 | H4 | H4 | H4 |
| H5 | | | | | H5 | H5 | H5 | H5 | H5 | H5 | H5 | |
| H6 | | | | H6 | H6 | H6 | H6 | H6 | H6 | H6 | | |
| H7 | | | H7 | H7 | H7 | H7 | H7 | H7 | H7 | | | |
| H8 | | H8 | H8 | H8 | H8 | H8 | H8 | H8 | | | | H8 |
| H9 | H8/H9 | H8/H9 | H8/H9 | H8/H9 | H8/H9 | H8/H9 | H9 | | | H9 | | H9/H10 |
| H10 | H9/H10 | H9/H10 | H9/H10 | H9/H10 | H9/H10 | H10 | | | | H10 | H1/H10 | H1/H10 |

**Figure 21:** Table of the prevalent energy of Year Flow on Heavenly Stem

| Month | Feb | Mar | Apr | May | Jun | Jul | Aug | Sep | Oct | Nov | Dec | Jan |
|---|---|---|---|---|---|---|---|---|---|---|---|---|
| | E3 | E4 | E5 | E6 | E7 | E8 | E9 | E10 | E11 | E12 | E1 | E2 |
| | 2/4 | 3/5 | 4/5 | 5/5 | 6/5 | 7/7 | 8/8 | 9/8 | 10/8 | 11/7 | 12/7 | 1/5 |
| E1 | E1/E12 | E1/E12 | E1/E12 | E1/E12 | E1/E12 | E1/E12 | | | | | E1 | E1/E2 |
| E2 | E1/E2 | E1/E2 | E1/E2 | E1/E2 | E1/E2 | E1/E2 | | | | | | E2 |
| E3 | E2/E3 | E2/E3 | E2/E3 | E2/E3 | E2/E3 | E2/E3 | E3 | | | | | |
| E4 | | E4 | E4 | E4 | E4 | E4 | E4 | E4 | | | | |
| E5 | | | E5 | E5 | E5 | E5 | E5 | E5 | E5 | | | |
| E6 | | | | E6 | E6 | E6 | E6 | E6 | E6 | E6 | | |
| E7 | | | | | E7 | E7 | E7 | E7 | E7 | E7 | E7 | |
| E8 | | | | | | E8 | E8/E9 | E8/E9 | E8/E9 | E8/E9 | E8/E9 | E8/E9 |
| E9 | E9 | E9 | E9 | E9 | | | E9 | E9/E10 | E9/E10 | E9/E10 | E9/E10 | E9/E10 |
| E10 | E9/E10 | E9/E10 | E9/E10 | E9/E10 | E10 | | | E10 | E10/E11 | E10/E11 | E10/E11 | E10/E11 |
| E11 | E10/E11 | E10/E11 | E10/E11 | E10 | E10 | | | | E11 | E11/E12 | E11/E12 | E11/E12 |
| E12 | E11/E12 | E11/E12 | E11/E12 | E12 | E12 | E12 | | | | E12 | E1/E12 | E1/E12 |

**Figure 22:** Table of the prevalent energy of Year
Flow on Earthly Branch

For example, 2012 was the year of H9–E5. Based on Figure 21, the energy of Water of H9 of this year started from the Beginning of Spring (February) and ended on the White Dew (early September), lasting seven months in total. Then it started again on Great Snow and ended in the Slight Heat of the next year.

Also from Figure 21 we can tell that in the year of H9 from the beginning of Spring to the beginning of Autumn, the energy of H8 and H9 coexist (並氣, Bing-Qi). This means that both energies exist and are in effect.

On the Earthly Branch side, the year 2012 was the year of H9–E5, the energy on Earthly Branch was E5, which started on April 5 and ended November 7.

From the figures, we can also see that during some months the energy of Year Flow is absent. During this period no energy comes into effect. For example, the year 2010 was the year of H7–E3. Between November (E12) and January (E2), there was absolutely no energy from the Year Flow. During this period we only need to analyze the effect of Grand Fortune and Month Flow, since there is no energy present on Year Flow.

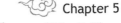 
# Section 2
# How to integrate Grand Fortune, Year Flow, and Month Flow into the analysis along with the Four Pillars

To analyze the fortune of a person of a given month, we need to consider the Four Pillars, Grand Fortune, Year Flow, and Month Flow together. Here are the guiding principles of the analysis:

1. Heavenly Stems and Earthly Branches should be analyzed separately.

2. First of all, we need to see if there is any coupling among Grand Fortune, Year Flow, and Month Flow. Those energies that coupled with others will lose at least partially their power to influence others.

3. We then look at whether there is coupling/transformation between any of the Grand Fortune, Year Flow, and Month Flow, and any of the Four Pillars. Such coupling/ transformation will change the original dynamics among the Four Pillars and can be used to indicate likely events.

4. Next, we check if there is any production or countering among Grand Fortune, Year Flow, and Month Flow. If there is countering, we need to see if any element in the Four Pillars can bridge it.

**5.** Lastly, we check if there is production or countering relationship between any of the Grand Fortune, Year Flow, and Month Flow, and any of the Four Pillars. If there is countering, check whether bridging exists.

Let's take Figure 23 as an example. Within the Four Pillars, there is no Officer Countering Peer. But when H2 appears either in Grand Fortune, Year Flow, or Month Flow, there could be serious events of Side Officer countering Main Peer. For example:

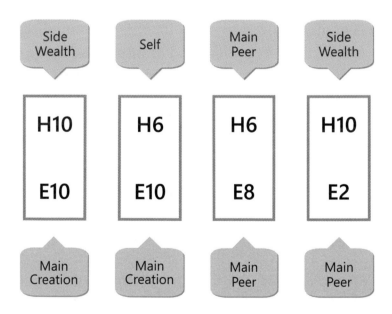

**Figure 23:** An example of a BaZi Chart

🔹 During the month as shown in Figure 24A—we first look at the interactions among Grand Fortune, Year Flow, and Month Flow. The Year Flow of H10 produces H2 both on Grand Fortune and Month Flow. Among the Heavenly Stems of the Four Pillars, there is no energy of Creation (Metal) that could counter H2, nor is there any energy of Empowerment (Fire) to help to bridge. As a result, there is serious Side Officer countering Main Peer.

🔹 Also, both H9 and H10 coexist in the Monthly Flow. H9 also enhances the energy of H2. So the likely events of Side Officer countering Main Peer, such as accidents, being backstabbed, pressure from work or being bullied may occur. It is also possible to have health issues related to countered Earth (H6). Although on the Earthly Branch side the energy of Creation counters Side Officer and may somewhat help the situation, the person still needs to be very careful about the potential events indicated by the Heavenly Stem side.

🔹 If the person encounters the month as shown in Figure 24B, again we first analyze the interactions among Grand Fortune, Year Flow, and Month Flow. H2 produces Side Empowerment of H4. As a result, the same power of H2 in this scenario facilitates Officer Producing Empowerment. The Month Flow of E8 counters the Year Flow of H12 (Main Wealth). But E8 as yin Earth is not effective countering the yang Water of E12, and the E2 in the Four Pillars clashes against E8, reducing its countering power. The Metal of E10 in the Four Pillars also is not effective producing H12 on the Year Flow. Since the interaction between Year Flow and Month Flow are closer and stronger than that between Year Flow and the Four Pillars, the person should still pay attention to his spending and wealth management.

🜄 Under the month as shown in Figure 24C, this is the year of H4/E12 and the month of H5/E9. The energy of Year Flow is empty on the Earthly Branch side during this month.

We first look at the interactions among Grand Fortune, Year Flow, and Month Flow. H2 produces H4, which then produces H5. H5 is where the energy is concentrated.

We then have to pay attention to the coupling of H5/H10. In the previous chapter we mentioned that in the event of H5/H10 coupling, with no transformation taking place, H10 is seriously damaged. In this case, H10 is not transformed into Fire, and H5 is where energy is concentrated, so H10 as Side Wealth is seriously damaged. The person needs to pay special attention to his spending and money management. Since this sign is on the Heavenly Stem side, it implies that the event may be public and known by others.

At the same time, the energy of Creation is strong on the Earthly Branch side. This is also a piece of information the person should be aware of.

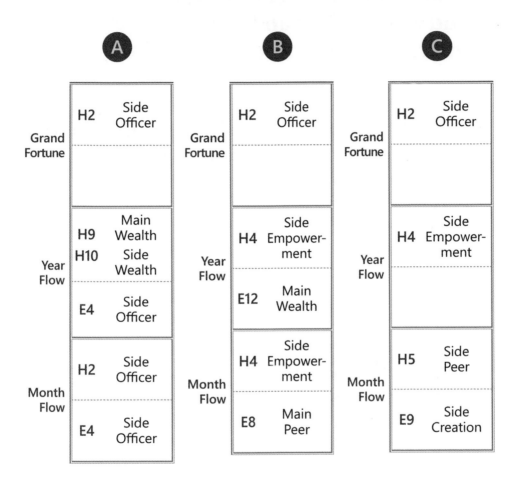

**Figure 24:** An example of Grand Fortune,
Year Flow, and Month Flow

# Section 3
## Grand Fortune, Year Flow, and Month Flow and their interactions with the Four Pillars

In Section 2 of Chapter 4, we discussed interactions such as Production, Countering, Coupling, and Transformation among the Five Elements of the Four Pillars. In this chapter, we will expand it further into the interactions of the Five Elements, not just among themselves, but also with external energies such as Grand Fortune, Year Flow, and Month Flow. This is an extension of what we have discussed in Chapter 4, section 2. It is preferred that readers comprehend the concepts by applying what they learned in Chapter 4 rather than memorizing everything.

We can divide these scenarios into two categories—Production and Countering. Each category contains five scenarios. As mentioned, Heavenly Stems versus Earthly Branches, as well as yin versus Yang, are analyzed separately. The outcome could, therefore, be complicated. For example, in the same month, a person may show signs of gaining wealth on the Heavenly Stem and losing wealth on the Earthly Branch. In this case, this person may have a chance to both make and lose money in the same month.

First, let's walk through the scenarios of countering.

# Officers Countering Peers

Implication: the person is likely to get into situations under which he or she is controlled, disciplined, constrained, or even hurt.

- **Females:** opportunity to enter into a relationship or marriage. Generally speaking, with Main Officer, there is a greater chance of getting a better husband or boyfriend. With Side Officer, however, the opportunity of romance requires caution. I have seen many cases of women entering into a relationship with married men during such periods.

- **Males:** Opportunity to have a child.

- **Side Officer Countering Self or Main Peer:**
  - † Pushed around or pressured by superiors in the workplace; framed or backstabbed; stressed out; litigation, etc.
  - † Accidents; injuries; haunted in some cases.
  - † Under the influence of bad things (e.g., narcotics, etc.)
  - † Females: not able to say no to men or being harassed or even violated in some extreme case.

- **Main Officer Countering Side Peer**
  - † Being occupied by work, but generally at a manageable level. Less likely to be stressed.
  - † Occasionally get into litigations.

- If the countered Peer were countering Wealth, Wealth would be enhanced as a result of Officer Countering Peer. In this case, the person may gain money during the period.

How to resolve the situation: Be aware and keep alert. Donating blood or engaging in sports activities may also help to alleviate the risk level.

## Empowerment Countering Creation

Implication: The person's mental and intellectual powers are suppressed.

- Intelligence suppressed. Easy to be deceived or make the wrong decisions. Troubled by personal matters.

- Prone to accidents due to own negligence or carelessness, for example, car accidents or occupational hazards.

- Frustrated by saying the wrong words or doing the wrong things.

- Sedated. Does not like exercise. Slow in studying. Controlled by parents or seniors.

- Introvert, low self-esteem, depression.

- Hard to create wealth, as Creations also signifies sources of wealth.

- Females: hard to conceive, or risk during pregnancy.

How to resolve the situation: when feeling depressed or unable to think clearly, reach out to friends for advice. Exercise more and engage in outdoor activities or travels. Try to avoid major decisions, or consult friends and experts in advance.

## Creation Countering Officer

Implication: The person gets tired of being controlled, taking commands or following orders. As a result, the sentiment of rebelliousness or resistance may arise.

- Tired of one's job. Fights against his/her boss. Quits or loses a job. Business owners closing down their businesses.

- Females: May find his husband/boyfriend irritating. Some may consider breaking up or divorce. Others simply spend less time with their partner.

How to resolve the situation: try to be more patient at the workplace. Females should try to be more patient at home. Maintaining a long-distance relationship during the period may also help.

Overall, try to communicate more and take a softer position with others. Divert the energy to foster one's own hobbies or creative works, research, publications, etc.

## Peers Countering Wealth

Implications: As the name suggests, Wealth is at risk of being damaged.

- May lose money through failed investments or lending money defaulted by others.

- For some, low desire to make money or pursue material wealth. For others, increased desire to spend money.

- On the other hand, for students who need to focus and study, or those who need to meditate (monks, for example), this would be a good time, as people during this period tend to be more calm and tranquil.

- Males: may be more demanding to their wives/girlfriends.

How to resolve the situation: avoid aggressive or risky investments. Try to divert the energy through healthy spending or donations. Avoid lending money to others. Be very cautious when invited to any investment opportunity. Males should pay attention in getting along with their wives/girlfriends and try to be more sensitive.

## Wealth Countering Empowerment

Implication: The person normally gets mentally restless during this time. It is normal that they travel around or get occupied all the time. Hard to settle down mentally or physically.

- Great chance for traveling, relocating, or oversea/out-of-town assignments.

- Opportunity to change jobs, careers, or environments.

- Those in management or supervising positions may find themselves powerless. This is because the energy of Empowerment is countered (Officer with no Empowerment).

- Mentally and physically restless. Hard to find peace of mind.

- Students may be easily distracted and have a hard time concentrations. As a result, they may display poor academic performance.

- May gain unexpected wealth such as lottery winning, etc.

- Lack of sincerity or honesty (as the energy of Empowerment is broken). Immersed in playing. Lack of stability

- Value money over reputation or self-image. Some may choose to enter businesses not generally accepted by mainstream values (e.g., prostitution, mafia, pornography, etc.)

- Does not care about self-image. Lack of help from Noble Persons, does not get along with parents or parents are not well.

How to resolve the situation: divert energy into healthy activities such as traveling. Those at work may volunteer for business trips or expat assignments.

Now, let's discuss the scenarios of Production.

## Officer Produces Empowerment

Implications: Good fortune in careers. Gets help from Noble Persons. Has peace of mind.

- Gets a promotion or gains authority

- Performs well on the job. Recognized by superiors. Gains resources or opportunities to perform.

- Good timing for studying and getting degrees, as the person will put his/her mind into it.

- Making easy money as help comes from all sides. Those in the brokerage business (e.g., realtors, car or insurance sales) will find it easy to get deals. Some may get money through inheritance.

- Good time to purchase real estates.

## Peer Produces Creations

Implications: Intelligence and creativity are extremely strong. Inspired by ideas.

- Write books or articles. Make progress on research. Create and discover new things.

- Females: good probability to conceive and have children.

- For some, the accomplishments may be based on hobbies or interests.

## Creation Produces Wealth

Implications: Create wealth with own talents, intelligence, or creativity.

- Some create wealth via smart investments, others by getting additional jobs, paid projects, personal businesses, etc.

- Males: Good opportunity for meeting a girlfriend.

## Wealth Produces Officer

Implications: As the name suggests, the energy of the Officer rises. This is not a bad thing as long as Officer does not counter Peer.

- Have the desire or opportunity to take a managerial role in the organization.

- Females: Have the desire or opportunity to meet a boyfriend.

- Males: Good opportunity to have a child.

- Feel occupied by work (Main Officer) or stressed out (Side Officer).

- Occasionally get into legal battles or trouble.

## Empowerment Produces Peer

Implication: with the presence of Empowerment, this will be a fortunate period, with opportunity to:

- Make easy or passive income from stock dividends, commissions, etc.

- Inherit wealth

- Purchase property

- Get help from people

# Section 4
# Case Studies

## Case Study 1
## Ankylosing spondylitis

The client is a male born on April 24, 1989, hour of E2. He was suffered from Ankylosing Spondylitis during his graduate school years. As a result, he was relieved from his obligation of military service in Taiwan. His BaZi chart is shown in Figure 25:

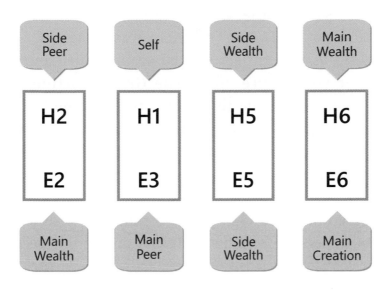

| Age | 7 | 17 | 27 | 37 | 47 | 57 | 67 | 77 |
|---|---|---|---|---|---|---|---|---|
| Grand | H4 | H3 | H2 | H1 | H10 | H9 | H8 | H7 |
| Fortune | E4 | E3 | E2 | E1 | E12 | E11 | E10 | E9 |

**Figure 25:** BaZi Chart for Case Study 1

The H1 and H2 in his BaZi chart is impacted whenever H7 or H8 is present. This is due to the Wealth (H5 and H6) in his chart strengthening the energy of H7 or H8. As we have covered, countered H1 or H2 implies health issue associated with either liver, ball gladder, tendon, bones, hair, or immune system. In this case, the client had Ankylosing Spondylitis.

In 2010, year of H7-E3. The client was at age of 22. The energy of H7 as Side Officer started around April and lasted till October (see Figure 26A). The Grand Fortune of H3 was supposed to be able to counter H7, but the H5 in the BaZi Chart bridged it. As the result, H1 as Self was for sure damaged. At the same time, H7 coupled with H2, and H2 was also damaged as the result. In this case, H7 represents Side Officer. This implies pressures at work (in this case, his study at graduate school). It turned out that he was under tremendous pressure from his professor during this period.

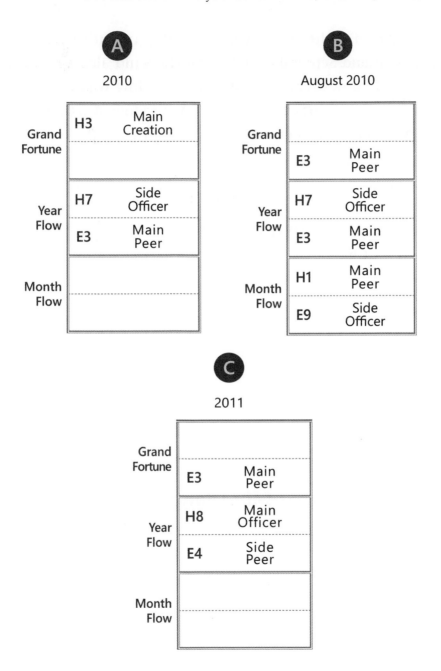

**Figure 26:** Grand Fortune, Year Flow, and Month Flow
in some specific periods

In 2010, in addition to April and May (month of E5 and E6), August and September (E9 and E10) could also be severe. Figure 26B shows August 2010. Month Flow was H1-E9, in which H1 was countered by H7 of Year Flow. Furthermore, E3 of Year Flow clashed with E9 of Month Flow. Countered Wood occurred on both Heavenly Stem and Earthly Branch. In September, H7 coupled with H2, and H2 was damaged as a result.

In 2011 (year of H8-E4) H8 of Year Flow countered H2 in the BaZi Chart (see Figure 26C). Adverse conditions may be present in February, March, July, December, or January of 2012. As Grand Fortune switched from H3 to E3 around August 2010, the countered Wood on the Heavenly Stem would become more severe. The severe condition could last till 2012 when the Water of H9 came into Year Flow.

## Case Study 2
## The affair of Chien-Min Wang

The birth date and time of Chien-Min Wang is March 31, 1980 at the hour of E11. Here is his BaZi Chart and Grand Fortune:

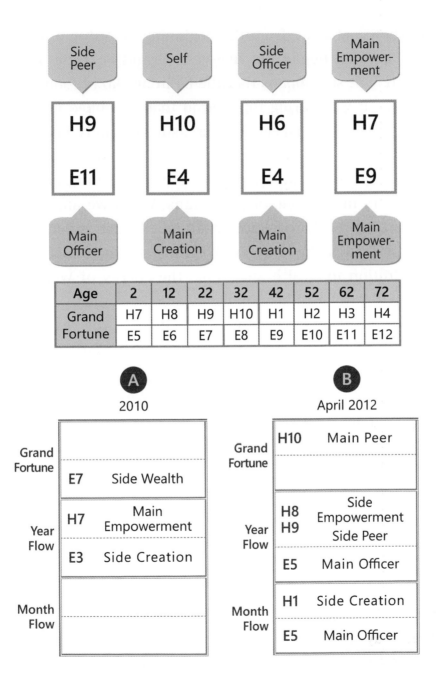

**Figure 27:** BaZi Chart of Chien-Ming Wang

As shown, starting from the beginning of Autumn in 2006 (age 27), Wang began his five-year Grand Fortune of Side Wealth (E7). It so happens that the E4 in his BaZi produces the Fire of E7. It was during this period that he gained fame and fortune in the Major League, increasing not only his wealth but also his number of fans. Wealth in BaZi refers not only to monetary wealth, but also fans, audience, subordinates, or even voters in the case of politicians. When we analyze the popularity of a celebrity, politician, or a leader among his or her subordinates, the energy of Wealth is our main focus.

In addition to wealth and fame, the energy of Wealth for men can also refer to his popularity among women. According to the press, Wang's affair took place in 2010 the year of H7–E3 (refer to Figure 27A). He was still in this Grand Fortune of Side Wealth, but that year he had an injury and was unable to play in the games. The energy of Side Wealth turned out to manifest in his affair.

Based on his Year and Month Flow of 2010, the E3 of Year Flow produces the Fire of E7, and at the same time clashes against the Metal of E9 in the BaZi Chart. E9 represents Main Empowerment in this Chart. As we have learned, Empowerment represents a sense of morality. Such a clash weakened the energy of Main Empowerment and, as a result, weakened Wang's sense of morality, making him easier to succumb to temptation.

One may argue that the energy of E3 is already vented or weakened by producing E7, but E3 being yang Wood does not really produce the yin Fire of E7 effectively, so its energy is mainly to clash against E9. With a strong energy of Side Wealth and weakened energy of Main Empowerment, Wang had an affair.

The energy of E3 started from the beginning of Spring in February and ended in August. Although Side Wealth of E7 was still strong, Main Empowerment of E9, without clashing against E7, was restored. We could assume so was his sense of morality. The energy of Wealth continued in October and November (months of E11 and E12), as the Heavenly Stem of these two months were H3 and H4; both were the energy of Wealth.

The incoming energy of the beginning of Winter and Great Snow contains the Water of E12 and E1, which severely countered the energy of E7. With the energy of Wealth subsided and Empowerment restored, we analyzed that the affair that started in February probably ended around November. This is basically inline with Wang's statement in the press (that the affair lasted about eight months).

The next year (2011), Year Flow was H8-E4. During the months of H7-E3, H8-E4, H10-E6, H1-E7 (February, March, May, and June), the energy of Creation Producing Wealth is present. It is possible that remnants of the affair were still present during this period. In the press, Wang said that he still kept in touch with his mistress the year after their affair ended. He may be referring to these months.

Wang's BaZi shows the strong energy of Creation on his Earthly Branch. This implies that whenever he encounters Wealth on the Earthly Branch side, whether it's in his Grand

Fortune, Year Flow, or Month Flow, he has a good opportunity of making money. That said, the Fire of E6 in 2013 was not as good as the Fire of E7. Readers who studied the previous chapters should be able to figure out why. His affair was exposed to the public on April, 2012 (see Figure 27B). This is likely caused by the H6 of Side Officer coupling with the Month Flow of H1. The coupling enhanced Side Officer, which manifested into backstabbing (someone intentionally leaked the news). Luckily, Year Flow of H9 produces H1, and H1 was not damaged by the coupling. Damage by the incident was limited.

Furthermore, Main Empowerment on the Earthly Branch was still with him. Empowerment signifies protection offered by seniors. He had the support of the team management.

One additional note—Wang has a Side Officer next to Self. This implies that he needs to be careful with accidents and injuries. Based on the Month Flow, his injury in February, 2012, was mainly due to his negligence. Readers should be able to figure this out by now. If not, it would be better to take a pause here and review what we have learned earlier before moving on to the next section.

## Case Study 3
## No one believed what I said

My classmate was born on December 7, 1964, at the hour of E4. Here is his BaZi chart:

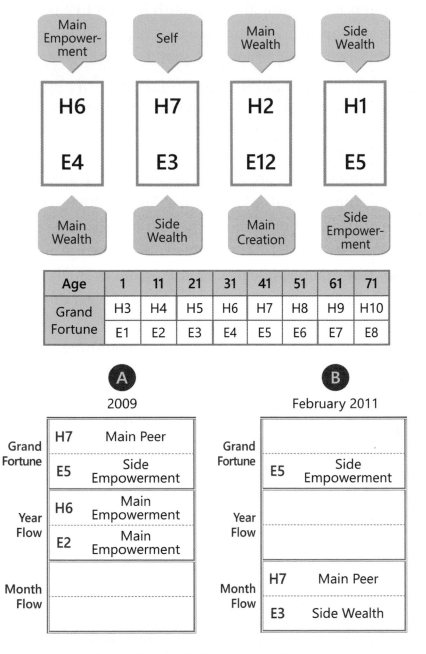

**Figure 28:** BaZi Chart of my classmate

In reference to Figure 28, the month branch E12 is coupled with the day branch E3. This makes E12 more vulnerable to countering from year branch E5. 2009 was the year of H6–E2 (see Figure 28A). Grand Fortune was H7 before Great Snow. After Great Snow, Grand Fortune changed to E5. Year Flow of E2 lasted from January of the previous year to July. As such, both E1 and E2 coexisted in Year Flow for seven months. Kidney issues are related to countered Water. It is not surprising that he had a kidney problem in 2009. 2010 was the year of H7–E3. As the Earthly Branch of Year Flow changed from E2 (Earth) to E3 (Wood), his kidney symptoms were relieved. Note that although Grand Fortune in 2010 was still E5 (Earth), E3 (Wood) in Year Flow counters E5, so this did not cause kidney problems.

2011 was the year of H8–E4. At the beginning of Spring (see Figure 28B), Year Flow was empty, so Month Flow really mattered. H7 coupled with H2 and countered H1 in the BaZi chart. As a result, both H1 and H2 of Wood were damaged. This was why I suspected the health issue was related to countered Wood (liver, bladder or the immune system). Furthermore, E3 of Wood in Month Flow countered E5 of Grand Fortune. Therefore, I was convinced that the issue was not caused by the kidney.

2012 was the year of H9–E5, with the energy of E5 starting from Pure Brightness. As the energy of E5 increased, kidney issues became more likely, especially during the months when Fire (Officer) was present in Month Flow, as Fire producing Earth will enhance the power of E5.

2013 was the year of H10–E6. With E6 of Fire and Grand Fortune still being E5 of Earth, E6 of Fire producing E5 of Earth makes Earth countering Water more serious. Kidney issues may be more serious. He needs to pay extra attention to his health.

## Case Study 4
## Never judge a person by their appearance

The young lady, in this case, was born on April 13, 1982, at the hour of early E1. Here is her BaZi Chart.

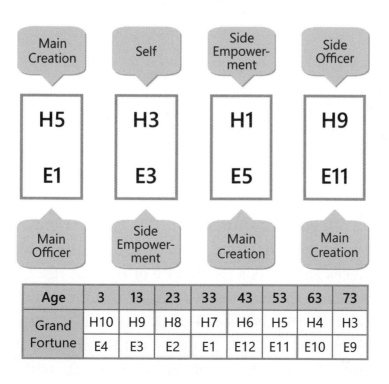

| Age | 3 | 13 | 23 | 33 | 43 | 53 | 63 | 73 |
|---|---|---|---|---|---|---|---|---|
| Grand Fortune | H10 | H9 | H8 | H7 | H6 | H5 | H4 | H3 |
| | E4 | E3 | E2 | E1 | E12 | E11 | E10 | E9 |

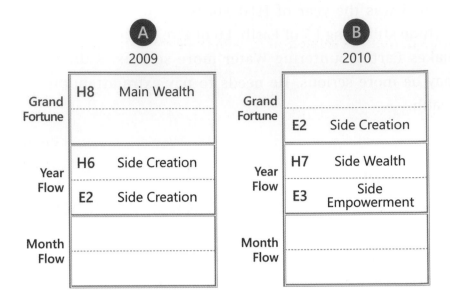

**Figure 29:** BaZi Chart of the young lady

In reference to Figure 29A, in 2009 (year of H6-E2) the energy of Year Flow H6 was present between the beginning of Summer and the beginning of Winter. H6 coupled with H1 in the Month Stem. Since H1 helps bridge H9 from countering Self, the coupling weakened H1, making Self more vulnerable.

H5 next to Self also offers protection against H9, but Grand Fortune of H8 couples with Self of H3. This not only makes H3 more vulnerable but also reduces the H3-H5 production (Fire produces Earth). As a result, Fire of H3 is at risk of being countered. Eye problems are a form of countered Fire. The risk was high during the month of H7, H8, and H9, especially during the month of H7-E7. Not only did H7 produce H9, but E7 was clashed against by E1 of the Hour Branch. With Water countering Fire happening both on Heavenly Stem and Earthly Branch, matters related to this were likely to happen.

Why the left eye? Because both Year and Month Stem are on the left side of Self (visualize that Self as facing us). With it, the lady should pay attention to her eyes whenever she encounters H6 (Grand Fortune, Year Flow, or Month Flow), especially during the ages of 43 to 48, when she undergoes five years of Grand Fortune of H6.

Figure 29B shows that Grand Fortune in 2010 was E2 (Side Creation). E2 coupled with E1 (Main Officer), the energy of Main Officer was suppressed as a result. This is why I assumed that she was not having too much luck with her relationships because of her temper. The Year Flow of E3 cannot suppress E2 because it is a yang-yin countering. In 2011, Year Flow of E4 could counter E2, but it could also cause depression (Empowerment countering Creation). In 2013 and 2014, as Fire in Year Flow produces E2, her temper in her relationship could flare up again.

Some practitioners say that Self cannot bridge Month Stem and Hour Stem. In this case, we can see this is not the case. The young lady worked in a high-tech company, and her boss and peers all thought that she was a smart and highly capable person. If Self does not help bridge H1 and H5, she would have had Empowerment countering Creation both on Heavenly Stem and Earthly Branch—not exactly the type of chart for a smart and capable person.

# Case Study 5
# It's not easy to read the chart of a relative

The family member, in this case, was born on July 12, 1973, at the hour of E10. Here is his BaZi Chart:

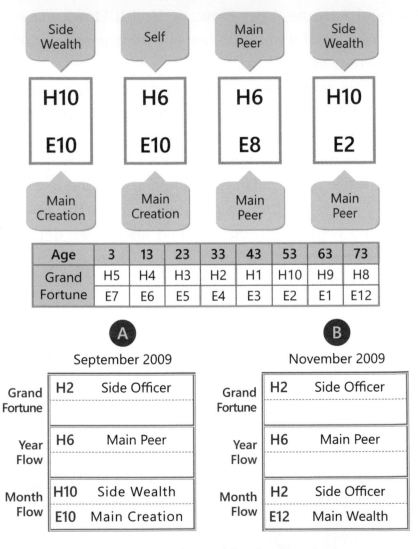

**Figure 30:** BaZi Chart of the family member

We already used this chart previously. Now, let's see how we can quickly capture the key points. The first thing that comes to mind is that he has only Peer and Wealth on the Heavenly Stem side. This implies he is totally defenseless in front of the energy of Officer, since there is no Empowerment (to do the bridging) nor Creation to counter the energy of Officer.

From March 2005 (age 33) he started his five-year Grand Fortune of H2 (Side Officer). As we mentioned, after analyzing the coupling, we should first look at the interactions among Grand Fortune, Year Flow, and Month Flow. Among the course of the five-year period, Year Flow on the Heavenly Stem side were H2, H3, H4, H5, and H6. Among these five Year Flow, H2 and H6 both made Side Officer countering Main Peer more serious, as H2 enhanced the energy of Side Officer, and H6 was directly countered by H2 as a result.

Let's take a look at the year of H6-E2 (2009). It's not difficult to tell that in May, August, September, October, and November (H6-E6, H9-E9, H10-E10, H1-E11, H2-E12), Side Officer countering Self was very severe (Main Peer of H6 being countered in the Year Flow is the same as Self being countered). The months of H10-E10 and H2-E12 were the worst (see Figure 30A/B).

The months when Officer countered Self in 2005 were the months of H6-E4, H10-E8, and H2-E10. Readers should be able to figure this out. Two additional notes to keep in mind 1) The energy of H2 came in two separate periods. Grand Fortune was changed to H2 from the Wakening of Insects, and the month of E2 at the end of the year was also subject to countering from Officer, but 2) that month both H2 and H3 were present. H3 is more or less able to bridge Side Officer of H2. H3 is not a very effective bridge (yin vs. yang), so the effect of Side Officer cannot be completely ignored.

Starting from 2010, the years of H7, H8, H9, and H10 were helpful to his business and personal wealth. In fact, his business did improve during those years.

## Case Study 6
## In memory of Echo

Echo was born on March 26, 1943, at the hour of E3. Here is her BaZi chart.

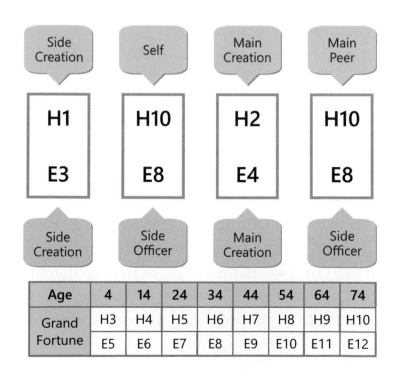

| Age | 4 | 14 | 24 | 34 | 44 | 54 | 64 | 74 |
|---|---|---|---|---|---|---|---|---|
| Grand Fortune | H3 | H4 | H5 | H6 | H7 | H8 | H9 | H10 |
| | E5 | E6 | E7 | E8 | E9 | E10 | E11 | E12 |

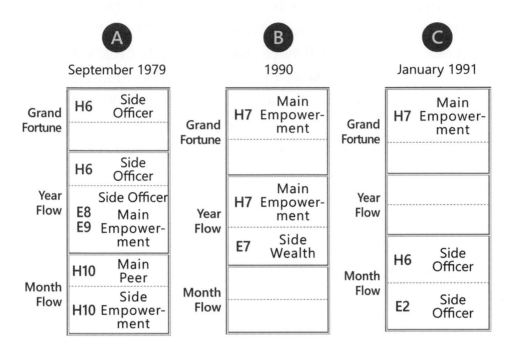

**Figure 31:** BaZi Chart of Echo

Between the ages of 29 and 34 (1971 to 1976), she was under Grand Fortune of E7 (Side Wealth). E7 coupled with her E8, which strengthened the energy of Fire (Wealth). Also, the E4 of her Month Branch produced Fire of E7. As a result, her Wealth energy was very strong during that period. It was during these years that she gained fame and popularity. Readers and fans are a form of Wealth. Echo made her name with her talent (Creation produces Wealth).

Such conditions lasted till age 46 (1988). Why 46 rather than 44 (1986)? First of all, her BaZi was very vulnerable against the energy of Empowerment, as Empowerment counters

Creation, which composes half of her BaZi (and her talent as a writer). In 1986, her Grand Fortune switched to H7 of Main Empowerment. H7 not only countered the Side Creation of H1 but also coupled the Main Creation of H2. Fortunately, Year Flow in 1986 and 1987 were H3-E3 and H4-E4. Both Fire of H3 and H4 countered the energy of H7, suppressing its power. After 1988, it would appear that the energy of Empowerment would create obstacles for Echo as a writer, as it suppressed her energy of Creation.

As for her personal life, her Grand Fortune turned to H6 of Side Officer in 1976 (age 34). Her husband's accidental death in September, 1979, can be seen on her chart (see Figure 31A). The Month Flow of H10 produced H2 on the Month Stem, which countered H6 of Side Officer (which represented her husband). Personally, I think such a tragedy did not have to happen. In my practice when I see a similar pattern on the chart of any female client, I would advise them to not have their husband engage in risky activities during the month, and maybe have them live separately for a short period.

As mentioned, the energy of Empowerment started to trouble Echo since 1988, which not only compromised her creativity but also triggered her depression. From public information, it is hard to tell when she started to show symptoms of depression, however it was during this period that she turned to religion. In my opinion, this is not the best remedy for her condition. Religion is a form of Empowerment, which could make her condition even worse.

1990 was a really bad year for Echo (see Figure 31B). It was the year of H7–E7. Both H7 on Grand Fortune and Year Flow caused serious damage to H1 and H2 on her BaZi chart. It is not hard to imagine that she had a rough time. Fortunately, the E7 of Fire on the Year Flow more or less suppressed the power of Empowerment, helping her to get through the year.

The energy of H7 on Year Flow ended in October. This should have been an improvement. But the Fire of E7 also ended in December. In January 1991 (see Figure 31C), the energy of Year Flow was empty. Month Flow was H6–E2. H6 enhanced the energy of H7. The energy of H6 started on December 31, 1990. Echo died on January 4, 1991, the day of H1–E11. With H7, enhanced by H6 suppressing H1, her depression was too much for her to bear anymore. Furthermore, H1 on her Hour Stem coupled with H6. Creation coupling with Officer implied that she was missing her late husband. The coupled H1 was even more vulnerable with the countering of H7. She finally was no longer able to overcome her depression and took her life that day.

In retrospect, if Echo had been accompanied by a friend (Peer, which could bridge Empowerment countering Creation), or gone traveling (going out is a form of Wealth, which counters Empowerment) she might have been able to get through the difficult time. Her Grand Fortune was not good between the ages of 44 and 64, but after 64, her Grand Fortune would switch to H9, which would have enhanced her Creation. Her inspiration would have come back to her again. Nevertheless, what is gone is gone. Only her works are left behind as memories of her life.

## Case Study 7
## Inescapable fate

The female client, in this case, was born on May 11, 1976, at Hour of E7. Here is her BaZi chart.

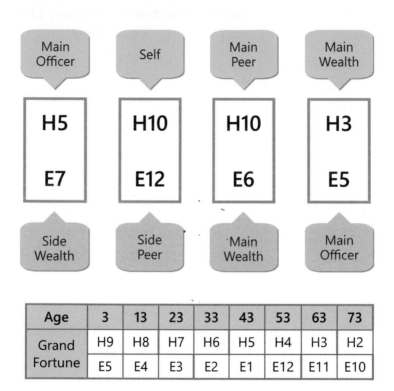

| Age | 3 | 13 | 23 | 33 | 43 | 53 | 63 | 73 |
|---|---|---|---|---|---|---|---|---|
| Grand Fortune | H9 | H8 | H7 | H6 | H5 | H4 | H3 | H2 |
| | E5 | E4 | E3 | E2 | E1 | E12 | E11 | E10 |

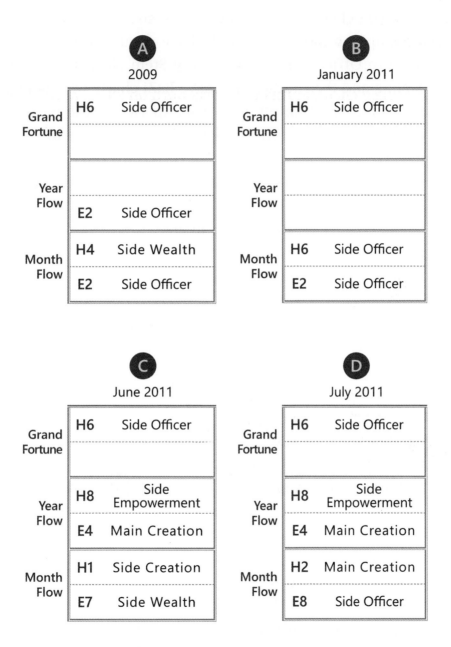

**Figure 32:** BaZi Chart of the female client

She and the client in Case Study 5 are sister and brother. If you compare their BaZi charts, both have a pattern that is very vulnerable to Officers on the Heavenly Stem side. In fact, her other sibling and their father also have BaZi charts with similar characteristics. Based on my personal experience, the patterns of BaZi can be passed on from parents to their children. Although the Five Elements may be different, once they are mapped to the Ten Spirits, I can often see the strikingly similar family resemblances.

The months of E4, E6, E10, and E2 in 2009 were all months with strong Side Officer. Figure 32A shows the month of E2 in 2009.

Some may wonder why she did not get pregnant in 2010. Year Flow was H7–E3. Not only E3 of Wood is her Side Creation, but E3 also couples with E12 of the Day Branch and transformed into Wood. The strong energy of Creation seemed to suggest good opportunity to conceive. But in reality, the energy of E3 came in along with E2 of Earth most of the time. Wood countered Earth suggested Creation countering Officer. As Officer implies husband, such countering reduced the chance to conceive.

In January, 2011 (as shown in Figure 32B), the prior three months (E11, E12, and E1) showed no signs of Creation anywhere. At the beginning of Fall, Month Flow of E9 clashed against the Wood of E3, and the energy of Wood showed no sign of revival. This explained why the baby's heartbeat stopped and the surgery in January, 2011.

Moving on to June and July of 2011 (see Figures 32C and 32D), when she conceived again, many BaZi practitioners may say it showed Empowerment countering Creation, which suggested the danger of miscarriage. But remember we always check coupling and transformation first. As H8 of Metal (Side Empowerment) coupled with H3 on the Year Stem, we generally do not consider it a serious threat to Creation. That said, in this case, Grand Fortune of H6 does produce H8, so the H8-H3 coupling did not fully constrain the energy of H8. The risk of countering should not be completely dismissed. In fact, her doctor did warn her about her of low placenta level. Readers should spend some time to think through this case, as it is rather complicated.

# Case Study 8
# Recovery from cancer

The client (born on August 3, 1971 at the hour of E6) has his BaZi chart as follows.

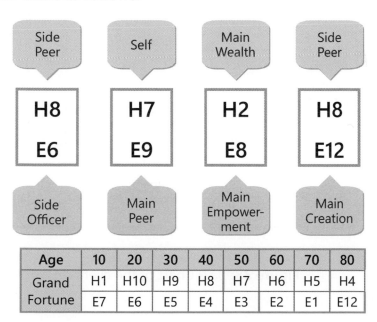

| Age | 10 | 20 | 30 | 40 | 50 | 60 | 70 | 80 |
|---|---|---|---|---|---|---|---|---|
| Grand | H1 | H10 | H9 | H8 | H7 | H6 | H5 | H4 |
| Fortune | E7 | E6 | E5 | E4 | E3 | E2 | E1 | E12 |

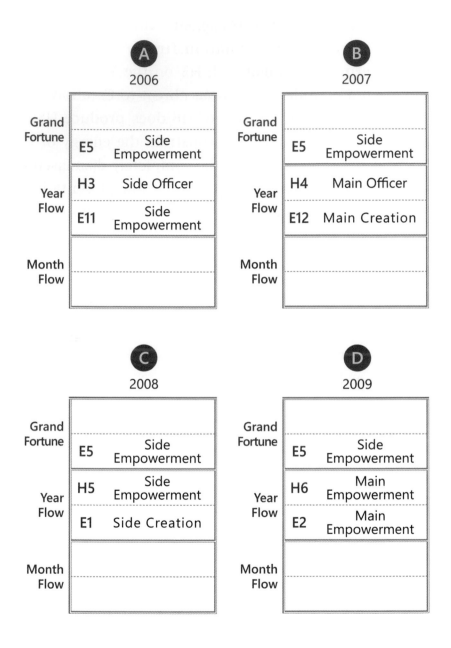

**Figure 33:** BaZi Chart of the client

202

In my experience, I've seen many cases of common physical issues related to the heart, liver, spleen, lungs, kidney, as well as hair loss, weight gain or loss, diabetes, stroke, and so on. I knew very well how to map these conditions on the Bazi charts. But this was the first time I encountered a case of nasopharyngeal cancer, so I had to investigate first.

It was very obvious that his weak spot in those years was on the E12 of Year Stem. In 2005 (age 35), his Grand Fortune switched to E5, which countered E12. I was convinced that his nasopharyngeal cancer was caused by countered Water. But as this was my first case study with this disease, I wondered if there was any support for my deduction. Looking up an old text on Chinese Medicine, I found that countered Water could cause symptoms in the head. I had read the text a long time ago, but at that time I thought "head symptom" meant something related to the ears, which I already knew. Looking at the text again made me wonder whether "head symptom" referred to something else, such as nasopharyngeal cancer.

In this case, E12 had been countered by E8 all along. Fortunately, the countering effect of yin Earth of E8 was weak against the yang Water of E12. But the countering from Grand Fortune of E5 starting from 2005 would cause serious damage. Possible symptoms of countered Water (urine bladder, kidney, blood, bone marrow, reproductive system, and in this case, nasopharyngeal issues) would likely occur.

Looking at Figure 33A-D, we see that from 2006 to 2009, E12 had been severely countered. 2009 was the year of H6-E2. Both H6 and E2 are Earth. H12 of Water was heavily countered. Based on the timing when the energy of E2 entered, it would have been most severe between January and July of 2009, and started to get better from February, 2010, with the entering of E3 of Wood. In August, the Month Flow of E9 entered, which produced E12. This would further improve the situation. However, in 2012 (year of H9-E5) between April and November, the problem could reemerge. In fact, it could emerge whenever E11 or E5 is present.

In addition to his physical condition, I suspected that the client also suffered from depression. His brother confirmed that it was the case, and in fact, the condition was quite serious. Depression is a common sign of Empowerment countering Creation, while physical diseases such as cancer are a result of prolonged countering in one's BaZi. As long as we can figure out the interaction between one's BaZi, Grand Fortune, and Year Flow, it is not difficult to predict the timing of his health condition going forward.

## Case Study 9
## Should he take the role of CEO?

The birth date and time of the client are March 16, 1976, at the hour of E6. Here is his BaZi Chart.

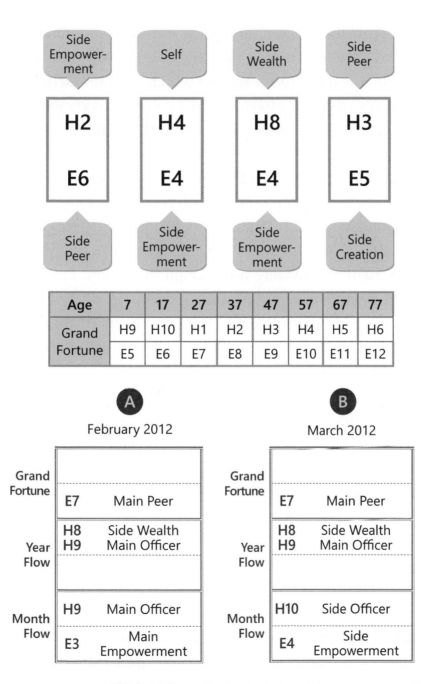

**Figure 34:** BaZi Chart of the client

Upon first look, the client does not have any Officer in his BaZi Chart. But notice that the H3-H8 coupling would transform H3 into H9 of Water, which is Main Officer. So it is not surprising that he would take a management role. That said, whether he was able to take the leadership role of an established company would require support from Grand Fortune, Year Flow, and Month Flow.

2012 was year H9-E5. Main Officer of H9 started from the end of January (see Figure 34A/B). Furthermore, H9 can produce H2 of Side Empowerment, making Officer producing Empowerment. If that were not enough, the Month Flow of the following months were H9-E3 and H10-E4. The sign of Officer producing Empowerment could not have been stronger. This was why I was so confident that the role of CEO was his to take even before I talked to him.

The energy of H9 finished in August. The following three months might be a bit bumpy. I advised that he should empower those he trusted to share his burden during this period. From the end of 2012, both energies of H9 and H10 came in. H10 is more effective producing H2 than H9 is. His career as CEO should have gotten even better. Such a situation would last till May 2014. Afterwards, the energy of Empowerment would remain strong for another few years.

[Note: This case example was written on April, 2013. In June, 2014, I was informed that the client left his CEO position, which was consistent with what I had predicted. His BaZi suggested that he still has a lot to expect from his career. I wish him all the best in his future endeavours.]

# Case Study 10
# Accidents that happened to me and my student

The BaZi chart (born on February 8, 1979, at the hour of E6) is shown here.

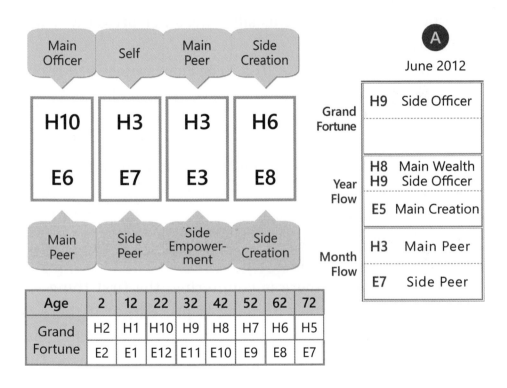

**Figure 35:** BaZi Chart of one of my PhD students

He was 32 years old. Grand Fortune of H9 of Water started from April, 2010. Throughout this and the next year, H7 and H8 on the Year Flow enhanced the Side Officer of H9 (see Figure 35A).

Physical problems are usually the result of countering for a prolonged period. In this case, the countering lasted for about two years. Also, I would assume that he had been quite stressed during this period. Those who are under the influence of Officer Countering Self usually encounter pressure, if not accidents or disputes, .

Starting from February, 2012, Year Flow switched to H9 of Water. During April and May, the Heavenly Stem of Month Flow (H1 and H2) could protect Self. In June, however, Month Flow switched to H3 of Fire, which was directly countered by H9. Some may think that H3 on the Month Flow should enhance Self, but remember that the interactions among the external energies such as Grand Fortune, Year Flow, and Month Flow always take precedence. The countered H3 of Month Flow is the same as countered H3 of Self.

Once we confirm there is countering, the first thing we should check is whether bridging is present, or if there is any energy that can counter H9. The first that catches our attention is H6 on the Year Stem, but H6 is yin Earth. The countering effect against H9 of yang Water is very weak. Also, Year Flow was both H8 and H9. H8 of Metal bridged such countering. In this situation, H3 was countered without any protection. As a result, accidents or physical issues related to Side Officer countering Self are likely to occur.

Furthermore, we can figure out when his thesis will be published. E5 of Year Flow starting in April were produced by E6 and E7 in May and June. E5 of Earth represents Main Creation. It is not surprising that his creation (thesis) got published.

My student got married in October 2016. As an exercise, readers may try to analyze and figure this out.

As for myself, although I also have H3 as Self, and was under the same Year/Month Flow, my Grand Fortune at that time was H10 of Main Officer. At the same time, H4 in my BaZi Chart coupled with H9. Although H4-H9 coupling caused no damage on either side, the energy of H9 is constrained. As a result, nothing serious happened to me. That said, I did feel some pressure at the workplace. So I still took extra precautions and donated blood that month to minimize the effect of countering.

# Case Study 11
# Troubled students born in the same month

My wife teaches at an elementary school. In the year 2012, there were two classes in the fourth grade. For some reason, she felt that both classes were particularly more difficult to manage than those in the previous years. Each class had a few difficult students. Some kept breaking the rules and ignoring their teachers; others could not sit still for five minutes and had a hard time staying focused. There were also more cases of bullying than usual.

One day, she had just finished grading a test. While she was uploading the scores, something caught her attention. The student numbers of most of these difficult students happened to be among the first few of their classes. In her school, student numbers are assigned in the order of their birth dates. She started to wonder whether their behavior had something to do with their BaZi.

We discussed this at home. I believed BaZi had something to do with their behavior. She had her reservations, as the behavioral issue of each student was quite different.

Based on the public education system in Taiwan, the birth dates of fourth-grade students range from September, 2001 to August, 2002. So the oldest students among fourth-graders would have been born in early September, 2001.

The BaZi of these students would have H8–E6 as the Year Pillar and H4–E10 as the Month Pillar. Putting both pillars side-by-side, it is obvious that H4 counters H8, and E6 counters E10. Both are Fire countering Metal. Although most people can find countering in their BaZi chart, countering of the same elements on both Heavenly Stem and Earthly Branch sides is not considered a good sign unless such countering is bridged or relieved.

If these students were born on the days of H1 or H2 (H1 or H2 as Self), then Fire countering Metal translates to Creation countering Officer. Students with such a BaZi, although they could be quite talented, usually have a strong personality and can be quite defiant against authority. It is not surprising that they do not like to follow rules or listen to their teachers.

For those who were born on the days of H5 or H6 (H5 or H6 as Self), the countering translates as Empowerment countering Creation. Such students tend to be more restrained, low energy, and have difficulties staying focused.

For those who were born on the days of H7 or H8, the countering translates as Officer countering Self. These students may fall victim to bulling more easily than others.

For those who were born on the days of H9 or H10, the countering translates as Wealth countering Empowerment. These kids could be hyperactive. Teachers would find it difficult to have them sit still. They may also be more likely to tell lies.

Countering between the same elements that take place on both Heavenly Stem and Earthly Branch of Year and Month Pillar is not common. Readers can go through the perpetual calendar to check. Even if this happens, it may or may not spell trouble. For example, those who were born in August, 2011, would have Year Pillar as H8-E6 and Month Pillar as H3-E9. It is also Fire countering Metal on both Heavenly Stem and Earthly Branch. But in this case, H3-H8 coupling and E6-E9 coupling could transform both H3 and E6 into water (just like Case Study E in Chapter 4). The outcome can be very different.

# Case Study 12
# Can BaZi be used to help
# make major decisions?

A reader once posted the following question to my web blog:

*"Dear Professor Hwang, I am wondering if you could help me with a question. My husband and I live in Vancouver. We are thinking of buying a house but are not sure if it is a good idea. We read some news articles that said the real estate market in Vancouver is a bubble. May I ask your opinion? When would be good timing for us to buy a house? Thank you."*

I replied to her as follow:

*"Dear XXX.*

*The fortune of a person throughout his life is affected by external factors. Regarding your question about buying a house, I would advise that you avoid making such a decision when your BaZi shows Empowerment countering Creation, or countered Wealth. The former could be a sign of poor judgment and a tendency to make the wrong decisions, while the latter could be a sign of loss of wealth.*

*In my opinion, so long as you are under the right BaZi condition, you could have a clear mind to make the right*

*decision, regardless of market conditions. This is how BaZi could help you. You may seek consultation from a professional BaZi practitioner. But be careful with those who ask you to pay to "change your fortune," for these are mostly scammers. If you need my further assistance, you are welcomed to send me an email. Thank you."*

Here I would like to discuss what BaZi can or cannot do to help us. Is the real estate market in Vancouver a bubble? If I had the BaZi of the person in charge of the real estate market I might be able to do some analysis. But any analysis from this would be tangential at best. BaZi mainly centers on individuals. It mainly tells the rise and fall of a person's fortune throughout their lifetime. BaZi is not used to predict macro market condition.

While BaZi does not offer much information on market conditions, it can help individuals make better decisions. I believe that there are people making money in the bear market, and people losing money in the bull market. Those who know their fortune and make the right decisions at the right time will likely fare better than others, regardless of how the market performs.

To advise clients on major decisions such as buying a house, I will usually look at the BaZi charts of the decision makers. If the decision is to be made by both husband and wife, I will read both their BaZi Charts. If other family members are also in the decision-making process, I will need their BaZi charts as well.

With all the BaZi charts of the decision makers, I will have to analyze them one-by-one to see if any of them shows sign of making the wrong decision (Empowerment countering Creation), or loss of wealth (countered Wealth). Based on the individual situations and the relationship among the decision makers, I may also need to check other factors. Making such analyses involving multiple parties requires a lot of skill and experience on the part of the BaZi practitioner.

The advice I give during consultations is usually about "who" should decide (best and worst person to make a decision), and "when" to decide (best and worst time to make a decision). As for the decision itself, whether it is to buy or not to buy, where to buy, which one to buy, and at what price to buy, is really up to the decision maker. I believe that it is not, and should not be my place to answer these questions in my BaZi consultation.

I believe that BaZi is a powerful tool that helps people make better decisions. But it is not without limitations. A good practitioner should know what BaZi can and cannot answer, and be open and honest about such limitations in his practice. I have seen many cases in which practitioners used unproven methods or provide advice that is beyond the limit of BaZi. I personally think this is highly irresponsible. A professional BaZi practitioner should stick to what he knows and advise accordingly. Any bad or wrong advice would have a profound impact on the lives of the clients. One must simply be very careful.

# Case Study 13
# Transformed Month Branch

Previously, we discussed whether Month Branch could be transformed. There are different opinions on this topic. Figure 36 is from a client of mine. Based on the rules we discussed in Chapter 3, Section 7, without any presence of E9 or E10, the E1-E2 coupling would transform E1 into yin Earth. But in this case, E1 is Month Branch. Normally, Month Branch is strong and hard to be transformed. This is why we rarely see cases wherein Month Branch is transformed. Some believe that Month Branch simply does not transform.

In this case, however, there are two E7 of Fire that produce E2. The energy of E2, enhanced by two E7 of Fire, is extremely strong. Therefore it does transform E1 into Earth. The transformation can be confirmed after verifying extensively with the client's personality as well as past events.

Transforming the Month Branch requires many conditions. Coupling must be present, the Month Stem needs to be with the right element, and the counterpart of the coupling needs to be very strong. These are indeed rare combinations.

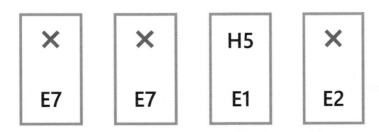

**Figure 36:** Example of Transformation on Month Branch

# Case Study 14
# Transformation affected by Year Flow

We have discussed this case in Chapter 4 (case E). Normally H3–H8 coupling would transform H3 of Fire into H9 of Water. But when the energy of H1 or H2 is present, the energy will produce H3 and make it revert back to H3, which is Side Officer in this case. The client, in this case, is a student. In October, 2014 (month of H1–E11), the energy of H1 started. I advised the client's parents to pay attention to his safety. Still, he got injured a few times in school. Luckily, it was nothing too serious (see Figure 37). In December, 2014, not only H1 and H2 of Year Flow reversed the transformed H3, but the Month Flow was also H3.

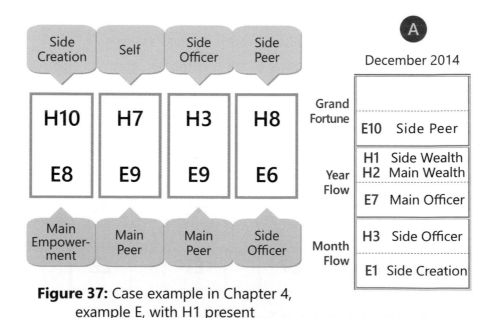

**Figure 37:** Case example in Chapter 4, example E, with H1 present

# Case Study 15
# The death of Corporal Hong

The accidental death of Corporal Hong was among the most impactful social news in Taiwan in 2013. Army Corporal Chung-Chiu Hong was going to be discharged from obligatory military service on July 6. Instead, he was found dead on July 4, just two days before he could go home. The suspected bullying and abuse, which caused his death, by his superiors soon turned this accident into a high-profile scandal and resulted in public outcry, demanding a thorough investigation and military reform.

Corporal Hong was accused of carrying a mobile phone (with camera function and an MP3 player) into the military facility and violating security protocol as a result. He was hence punished with confinement. On July 3, the weather temperature exceeded the regulated limit for conducting routine physical training. For some reason, Hong's superior officers and the guards of the brig still commanded him to do intensive physical training. After gruelling physical activity under high temperatures and with no chance to drink water, Corporal Hong soon showed signs of heat stroke. He had requested to stop but was denied. His condition soon got a lot worse. By the time he was sent to the hospital, it was already too late.

Based on the information on the Internet, Corporate Hong was born on September 8, 1988. We cannot find his hour of birth. His BaZi Chart is shown in Figure 38. In June, 2013, his

Grand Fortune was H7. The Year Flow was H9/H10–E6, and the Month Flow was H5–E7. Putting his BaZi Chart aside, the H5–H10 coupling and the H5 countering H9 between the Year Flow and Month Flow both indicate that the energy of Water (in his case, Creation) is damaged. As we have learned, Empowerment countering Creation indicates a tendency towards carelessness, making wrong decisions or saying the wrong words. Some of Corporate Hong's comrades testified that Hong's punishment was in fact retribution, as he was trying to be a whistleblower on the eve of his discharge. Empowerment countering Creation could indicate that he did not clearly consider the potential consequences.

In addition, both Main Officer (E6) and Side Officer (E7) were present on the Year Flow and Month Flow. This could indicate accidents, pressure from superiors, disputes, or being framed by others. The energy of Officers peaked between June 20 and July 3. Hong died on July 4.

The Science of BaZi Analysis: Grand Fortune, Year Flow, and Month Flow

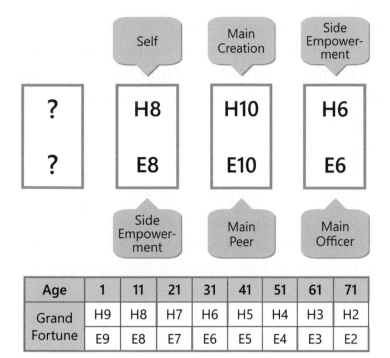

| Age | 1 | 11 | 21 | 31 | 41 | 51 | 61 | 71 |
|---|---|---|---|---|---|---|---|---|
| Grand Fortune | H9 | H8 | H7 | H6 | H5 | H4 | H3 | H2 |
| | E9 | E8 | E7 | E6 | E5 | E4 | E3 | E2 |

**A**

June 2013

| Grand Fortune | H7 | Side Peer |
|---|---|---|
| | | |
| Year Flow | H10 | Main Creation |
| | H9 | Side Creation |
| | E6 | Main Officer |
| Month Flow | H5 | Main Empowerment |
| | E7 | Side Officer |

**Figure 38:** The BaZi of Corporal Hong and the overall Fortune in June 2013

According to the press, Corporal Hong was outspoken and had a sense of righteousness. He openly made some comments that eventually got him in trouble. His Main Creation (H10) is strong. Main Creation counters Side Officer. It is in his nature to fight against injustice and oppression. But with Empowerment countering Creation, and Side Officer countering Self in June, it was bad timing for him to speak up. Usually, I would simply advise my client to keep a low profile and be careful under similar circumstance. In many cases, these clients told me afterward that they did avoid disasters that would have otherwise befallen them. The death of Corporal Hong was tragic. One can only take comfort in knowing that his death triggered a series of reforms in the military justice system and hoping that the same thing won't happen again.

## Case Study 16
## Is everything predestined? The BaZi of twins

People who study BaZi or another art of destiny often wonder whether a person's life is predestined and whether twins, who were born at an almost the same time and are with the same gender, would share the same destiny. Would they be destined to get married at the same time, with the same number of children, walk the same paths of life, and die at the same time? This is obviously not the case. BaZi provides a pattern of the life of a person, but it does not mean that everyone with the same BaZi will have the same destiny. We will discuss this further in Chapter 6. That said, studying the cases of twins would indeed help us with this question. Here I will provide two case examples of twins.

The first example is about a pair of twin brothers. They were born within the same hour and without a doubt share the same BaZi. The brothers have very similar personalities and tastes. They took the nationwide high-school evaluation tests and surprisingly got the same score. Although they chose to go to different colleges, both chose to major in physics. A while ago, their parents told me that both brothers wanted to transfer to an engineering major. I helped analyze the Year and Month Flow of the months before they took the transfer assessment exam and gave them some advice. I recently heard from their parents that each of the brothers was admitted to the school of engineering of different colleges. One will major in computer science and the other in electronics.

The other example was a father, who was a client of mine. His two daughters were identical twins, but they had not only very different personalities but also very different fates. One did very well at school, while the other not only did not perform well but suffered from depression at one point and had to drop out from school. Their father did not know why the fate of the twins could vary so much.

I told the father that my best guess would be that the two sisters were born at the change of hour, and therefore have different BaZi. He gave me their birth date and time, which was September 18, 1992, at around 9 a.m. 9 a.m. is right at the edge between the hour of E5 and E6. Once I laid out their BaZi chart, I asked their father if it is the younger sister who suffer from depression. He said yes.

In this case (see Figure 39 for the older sister, and Figure 40 for the younger sister), the BaZi of the younger sister indicated that indeed she was more vulnerable to depression. For the older sister, the countering of H1 against H6 was mild. Readers should recall H1–H6 coupling and understand the reason. In the case of the younger sister, however, H2 directly counters H6. Some may think that H4 helps bridge the countering. But the H4–H9 coupling constrained the power of H4, making it ineffective to bridge.

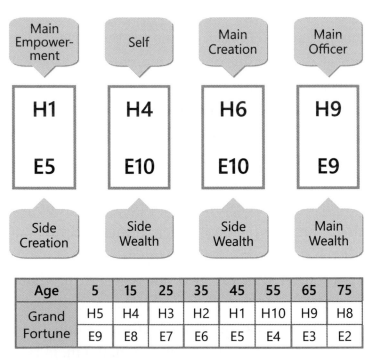

| Main Empowerment | Self | Main Creation | Main Officer |
|---|---|---|---|
| **H1** | **H4** | **H6** | **H9** |
| **E5** | **E10** | **E10** | **E9** |
| Side Creation | Side Wealth | Side Wealth | Main Wealth |

| Age | 5 | 15 | 25 | 35 | 45 | 55 | 65 | 75 |
|---|---|---|---|---|---|---|---|---|
| Grand Fortune | H5 | H4 | H3 | H2 | H1 | H10 | H9 | H8 |
| | E9 | E8 | E7 | E6 | E5 | E4 | E3 | E2 |

**Figure 39:** BaZi Chart of the older sister

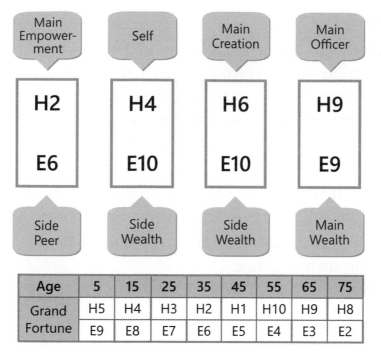

**Figure 40:** BaZi Chart of the younger sister

I will simply go straight to the conclusion of my analysis for the younger sister and leave the details to our readers. If you can come up with the same conclusion at ease, your BaZi skill would not be very far from being able to help others. The conclusion of my analysis suggests that she might have had a situation in 2012 after Chinese New Year (February). The situation or problem improved around August, then turned bad again around the end of December. It then got even worse around February and March of 2013. I asked her father if this was the case. He said her condition did get a lot worse in March, and in April the school informed him to take his daughter home.

With Empowerment countering Creation already in his BaZi, how do we tell the ups and downs of her condition? This is related to her Grand Fortune between the ages of 15 and 20, and the Year Flow of 2010 and 2011. Readers should also study the Month Flow of April, 2013, to understand why she dropped out of school that month.

Some schools of BaZi practitioners consider one's fate predestined. To explain away any difference between twins, they always put the Hour Pillar of the second-born using the next hour, regardless of their actual time of birth. I cannot agree with such a method.

## Case Study 17
## The life of Claude Monet

Claude Monet was the founder of the French Impressionism. A while ago, the National Museum of History in Taipei held a special exhibition of Monet's works that had been shipped from Paris. I am not an expert in fine art. To get the most out of the visit, I looked up the biography of Monet before my visit. Monet was born on November 14, 1840. Again, my curiosity as a BaZi practitioner drove me to look into his BaZi (See Figure 41). In front of me was the BaZi chart of a person who struggled to break free from the confines of convention, a person who put all his effort into achieving perfection, a person who struggled constantly with internal conflicts. It seems to me that such emotional conflicts were the driving force of Monet's creations.

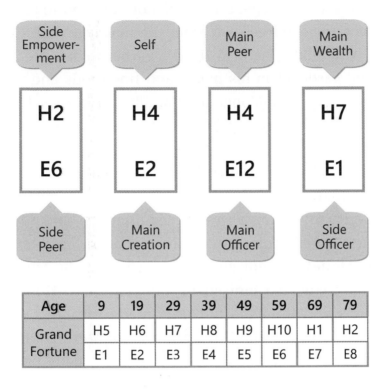

**Figure 41:** The BaZi of Monet

Monet's BaZi, from Year Pillar to Hour Pillar, is H7-E1, H4-E12, H4-E2, H2-E6, Here I derived his hour of birth by examining his biography and major events of his life.

On the Heavenly Stem side, H4 countering H7 shows Peer countering Wealth. This implied that his wealth came and went, and so could have been his marriage. Monet's first wife Camille died at the age of 32. This second marriage with Alice Hoschedé lasted longer. Monet had financial crises a few times in his life. Although he made quite some money selling his works of art, he also spent a lot. He not only had to support a family of eight children (two from the marriage with Camille, and six with Alice), he also lived a rather lavish life, with a nanny and gardener in his house and fine foods and wine on the dinner table. Both Monet and Camille were very selective in their choice of clothes. Camille used to order lots of clothes to pose for Monet. Also, all the travels that were required by his work also cost money. All these put a lot of pressure on his financial situation.

On the Earthly Branch side, E2 counters E1 and E12. This represents Main Creation countering both Main and Side Officers. Monet did not see eye-to-eye with the traditional school and dedicated himself to innovating art. His drive to break rules and innovate not only made him into what he was but also fits his BaZi of Creation countering Officer. A person with Creation countering Officer is usually conflicted within. He could feel both superior and inferior at the same time, which made him hardly satisfied and constantly strive to improve. He once said, "No one but myself knows the anxiety I go through and the trouble I give myself to finish the paintings which do not satisfy me and seem to please so very few others." Throughout his life, he destroyed hundreds of his works simply because he considered those works as failures. He even burnt over sixty of his paintings six months before he died.

Looking at the course of Monet's life, we see that his Grand Fortune between ages 9 and 14 was H5, which composed Creation producing Wealth. It was during this period that he started to build his initial reputation by selling his charcoal caricatures. Between ages 29 and 33 (nominal ages), he was under Grand Fortune of H7 as Main Wealth. In 1870, he had H7 as Main Wealth both in Grand Fortune and Year Flow and married his first wife, Camille, that year. In 1878, his Grand Fortune switched to H8. The two H4 in his BaZi started to counter H8. The countering situation remained in 1879. His wife Camille died from tuberculosis. Again, in 1911, (age 72), Grand Fortune was H1 and Year Flow was H8-E12. The two H4 in his BaZi countered H8. His second wife Alice passed away that year.

The energy of E3 or E4 would create Officer producing Empowerment for Monet. During such a period he was able to build his career. During ages 34 to 38, his grand Fortune was E3. E12 in his BaZi produced E3, which then produced E6, and E6 produced E2. In 1874, his work *Soleil Levant* (Impression Sunrise), exhibited in the first Impressionist exhibition, was a huge success and secured his position as a major impressionist artist. Between ages 44 and 48 (Grand Fortune as E4), he created numerous landscape paintings. His financial situation significantly improved, as his dealer, Paul Durand-Ruel was successful in selling his paintings at increasingly higher prices. In 1886, the Earthly Branch of Year Flow was E11 of Side Creation. Combined with the Main Creation in his BaZi, Monet's artistic style took a sharp turn. With much wilder strokes and colors, he made 39 stunning works.

Between ages 49 and 53, his Grand Fortune was H9. The H7 of his BaZi produced H9, making Main Wealth producing Main Officer. He was able to surpass himself and created a series of works, including *Les Meules*, *Les Peupliers*, and *Rouen*

*Cathedral*, thus securing his position as a grand artist.

Between ages 59 and 63, Grand Fortune was H10, which produced H2 in Monet's BaZi and, in turn, produced H4. Officer produced Empowerment, and Empowerment produced Self. In 1899, he began painting the *Water Lilies*, which became among the most well-known series of his works. But at the same time, H10 of water countered the H4 of Fire. He started to develop cataract. With his failing eye sight, his works also changed and became more blurry and abstract. H10 countering H4 started more than a year before 1900, but the H2 in his BaZi helped bridge the countering until 1900, which was the year of H7–E1. H7 coupled with H2, rendering the bridging ineffective. His eyesight started to fail.

From my perspective as a researcher of BaZi, I am amazed by how Monet's BaZi resonated with his life. The conflicts among the Five Elements created his internal conflicts and, at times, adverse environments, but they also kept driving and inspiring him towards creating timeless works of art.

## Case Study 18
## Lost and found

Analyzing one's fortune month-by-month requires a combined view of one's BaZi, Grand Fortune, Year Flow, and Month Flow. This is one of the most difficult parts of BaZi analysis. In Section 2 of Chapter 5, we summarized five guiding principles of analysis. One of the guiding principles is "analyze Heavenly Stem and Earthly Branch separately."

Since the book was published, many readers asked me what if the signs from Heavenly Stem and Earthly Branch contradict each other? For example, what if we have a case of Creation producing Wealth on the Heavenly Stem and Peer countering Wealth on the Earthly Branch?

My answer is simple—a person's life's journey seldom moves in one straight line. Contradictory things can happen simultaneously. It is not unheard of that someone makes money and loses money at the same time.

Here is a dramatic but real case example that supports my point. The client came to me in early 2014 to analyze his luck throughout the year. I told him to pay attention to the sign of loss of wealth in April (see Figure 42). In April, the Heavenly Stem showed sign of loss of Wealth, while the Earthly Branch showed a sign of creating Wealth. The client has H2 as Self and under Grand Fortune of E6. The Year Flow was H1-H10 and Month Flow was H5-E5. On the Heavenly Stem side, H1 of Wood countered H5 of Earth, representing Peer countering Wealth. On the Earthly Branch side, however, E6 of Fire produced E5 of Earth, representing Creation producing Wealth.

With this, I reminded him not to make any major investments between March 28 and April 14. Investments can be made with caution between April 15 and May 5.

On April 30, the client sent me a text message. He mentioned that he had a pending payment of over US$30,000 from a customer that he had not been able to collect. The customer had been avoiding him. If the money was not collected by the end of May, he would have to compensate for the loss from his own pocket.

This matches our analysis of loss of wealth. With this, I asked him if he had any investment plans in May, and he said no. I then told him "then it's good. Your BaZi shows a sign of creating Wealth in the second half of the month. It has not been fulfilled yet. I think you have a shot of getting the payment back by May 5. Try to be more proactive during this period."

On May 2, the client texted me again saying that he was able to find a way to collect the payment. With the strong sign of Creation producing Wealth, the client was able to create ways to recover his wealth. And I was happy to have had the opportunity to help.

As a side note, the H10 on his Year Flow represented Side Empowerment, which also implies Noble Person who could provide assistance. If he had asked for my advice after May 6, the Month Flow would have turned into H6-E6, and things would have turned out differently.

April 2014

| | | |
|---|---|---|
| Grand Fortune | E6 | Side Creation |
| Year Flow | H1 | Side Peer |
| | H10 | Side Empowerment |
| Month Flow | H5 | Main Wealth |
| | E5 | Main Wealth |

**Figure 42:** Grand Fortune, Year and Month Flow of the client

# Case Study 19
# Observing the energy in your day-to-day life

The energy of the Five Elements influences our daily lives, and we can reflect upon these influences to improve our BaZi reading. Here I would like to share some stories of my family.

My son's BaZi has H1 as Self (he is the example in Case D of Chapter 4, Section 4). The Self of H1 is unprotected. In 2016, he was under the Grand Fortune of E3. So the energy of H7 and E9 (Metal) is Side Officer to him, and the presence of this energy posed a big threat to him. Whenever the energy of H7 or E9 was present, he either got sick or got injured. So this year my wife and I have been reminding him to be careful.

My son is an avid cyclist. He had been riding all across Taiwan, challenging the most treacherous and demanding routes. This year (year of H3-E9 and month of H7-E3), in the first half of the month, the H7 of Metal was suppressed by H3 of Fire. But in the second half, the entrance of E3 of Wood would present a situation of Side Officer countering Self. The energy of E3 entered on February 14. In the afternoon of February 13 my wife and I were out on grocery shopping and we had just been talking about reminding our son once we got home. Just when we returned home and were about to open the door, we heard a loud noise of items falling to the ground, followed by a shriek. It was my son who stepped on the slippery floor and fell to the ground. We immediately opened the door and checked his condition. It took him a while to get up on his feet. Fortunately, he did not hit his head or any vital parts of his body, but he did twist his arm, get a big bruise, and break a toenail.

While my wife was treating our son's wound, I made a phone call to our daughter, who was in the college. Her voice over the phone was quite weak. She told me that she had a fever and a sore throat and that she had to take a day off from school. The physical condition related to Fire (H3) countering Metal (H7) was quite common that month amongst the people that I knew. Just a day before, while I was at a conference, the Chairman told me that he had had pneumonia triggered by sinusitis for a while. He had been trying a few different medications and still was unable to recover. My wife during that month had problems with constipation, and I was also coughing. All of these are common physical conditions of countered Metal.

February 14 was Day of H3-E3. The energy of E3 started from the hour of E11 (7pm-9pm) the night before. We cannot see or feel the energy, but it does affect us and can be observed through the events that happen around us. Although we were unable to prevent the accident that happened to my son, I am grateful that it was nothing serious. The energy effect always manifests in one form or another. The variable lies in the manner and extent of the effect. If we are aware of the possible effect and prepare ourselves for it, we should be able to reduce the damage. Since the same adverse energy in this example also affects the friends and family around us, it would be useful to pay more attention to these effects and the ensuing events. By doing so, it will not only improve our skills of BaZi analysis but enable us to help others as well.

# Case Study 20
# When disaster strikes: the six fallen heroes and the death of the famous director Chi Po-Lin

## A. The six fallen heroes

Those who doubt BaZi often ask "How do you explain major disasters when lots of victims die? Would it be possible that all of them suffered a bad fortune at the same time?"

This is a valid question. After all, what good is the art of BaZi or any art of destiny if it cannot even signal major disasters that could end a person's life? But major disasters such as plane crashes, tsunamis, or terrorist attacks like the September 11 attacks often involve hundreds or even thousands of victims. Is it possible that all of their BaZi showed signs of danger?

In my study of BaZi, I always take a logical and fact-based approach. This topic is no exception. But as it is next to impossible to get the birth date and time of every victim in a major disaster, I was not able to do anything with this topic.

In January, 2015, a vicious fire broke out in a bowling alley in Taoyuan, Taiwan. In an attempt to put out the fire, six firefighters lost their lives. In one news article, the birth dates of all six fallen heroes were listed. As tragic as it was, this presented me a never-before opportunity to study all the victims in one disaster.

Based on my experience, major disasters are usually related to accidents caused by strong Side Officer countering Peer, or

Empowerment countering Creation causing misjudgment. As I examined the BaZi of each fallen firefighter, it became clear that they all fit our theory. Amongst the six persons, four of them showed serious Side Officer countering Self, and three of them showed Empowerment countering Creation (one person showed both signs). In a dangerous situation such as the building on fire, the slightest mistake could cause serious consequences. Unfortunately, signs of danger showed on the BaZi of all six firefighters. Here we will examine them one by one.

## 1. Mr. Chang (born on March 9, 1993)

In his BaZi, the H10 produces H2 as Side Officer, which sits right next to Self. The Side Officer countering Self was strong to begin with. He was under Grand Fortune of H9, which produced the Year Flow of H1 as Main Officer. Moreover, H2 was also present in the Year Flow. The power of Officer was really strong.

The accident happened in the early morning of January 20, 2015, which was the second half of the month of H4-E2. The Month Flow of H4 was supposed to be able to mitigate the threat of H2, but the coupling of H4-H9 constrained the energy of H4, and, hence, it was not able to help fend off the Side Officer of H2.

The job as a firefighter is a highly risky one. People with strong Side Officer countering Self should be extra cautious undertaking such a career.

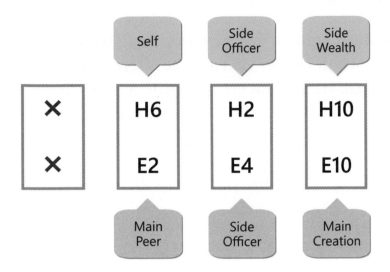

January 2015

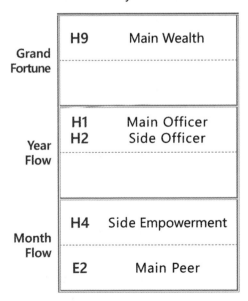

**Figure 43:** BaZi Chart of Mr. Chang

## 2. Mr. Chen (born on March 9, 1989)

Both Grand Fortune and Year Flow were H1 as Side Officer. H4 in the Month Flow is yin Fire. The effect of bridging for the yang Wood of H1 was not very effective. As a result, the sign of Side Officer countering Self was very strong.

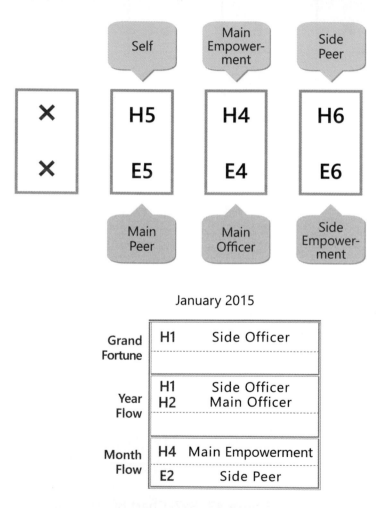

January 2015

| | | |
|---|---|---|
| **Grand Fortune** | H1 | Side Officer |
| | | |
| **Year Flow** | H1<br>H2 | Side Officer<br>Main Officer |
| | | |
| **Month Flow** | H4 | Main Empowerment |
| | E2 | Side Peer |

**Figure 44:** BaZi Chart of Mr. Chen

## 3. Mr. Tsai (born June 21, 1994)

On the Heavenly Stem side, the Self of H5 produced H7 of Main Creation, which countered H1 as Side Officer. It would appear that he was able to defend against the energy of Side Officer. However, Side Officer countering Peer still showed in the Earthly Branch side. What tipped the balance was the Year Flow of H1 and H2. The H2-H7 coupling constrained the energy of H7. As a result, both the H1 in his BaZi and the Year Flow directly countered Self.

There is another point. His Grand Fortune had just switched to E9 a few days before the accident. Before that, the last Grand Fortune of H9 had been producing H1 for five years. The energy of H1 was extremely strong.

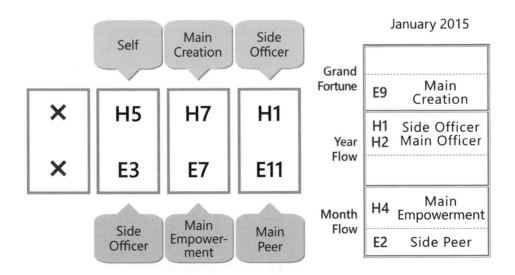

**Figure 45:** BaZi Chart of Mr. Tsai

## 4. Mr. Tseng (born on December 12, 1988)

It is clear in this chart that the Year Flow of H2 produced the Month Flow of H4, which is Side Officer. At the same time, Empowerment countering Creation (E2 countered E1) in his BaZi was enhanced by the additional E2 in the Month Flow.

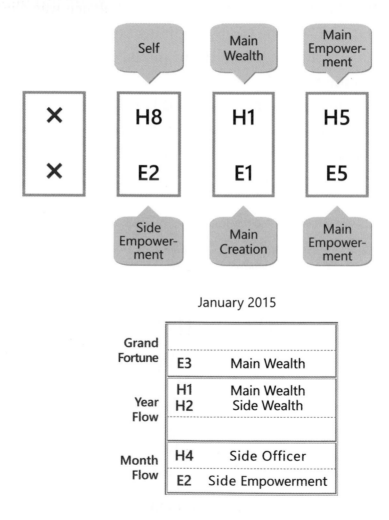

**Figure 46:** BaZi Chart of Mr. Tseng

## 5. Mr. Xie (born on September 15, 1986)

The Grand Fortune of H7 countered the H1 of Year Flow, and coupled with H2 of Year Flow. Both H1 and H2 as Creation are damaged. This signaled serious Empowerment countering Creation. Under the influence of such energy, it is hard for anyone to keep a clear mind and have good judgement. Usually, if I see such a condition during my consulting session, I would advise my client to avoid making any major decisions.

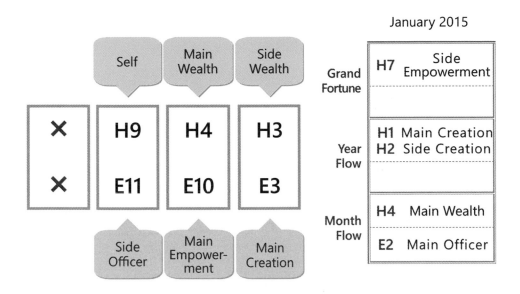

**Figure 47:** BaZi Chart of Mr. Xie

## 6. Mr. Chen (born on August 3, 1993)

The H6 in his BaZi was coupled by the H1 and then countered by H2 in the Year Flow. The situation of Empowerment countering Creation was severe. This caused him to not be able to react properly in front of any sudden dangerous situation.

One may wonder why the H4 in the Month Flow did not help bridge the countering. This may have something to do with his Hour Pillar. The reader may try to figure out what would be the possible Hour Pillar.

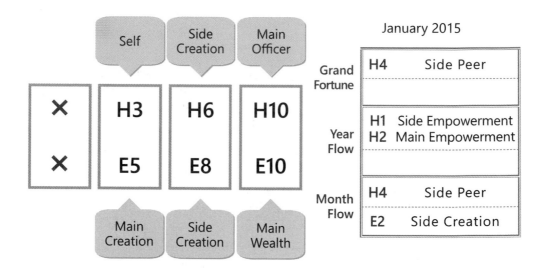

**Figure 48:** BaZi Chart of Mr. Chen

## B. The death of Chi Po-Lin

Chi Po-Lin is a famous director of documentaries in Taiwan. His most famous work "Beyond Beauty: Taiwan from Above" contained scenes of Taiwan's landscape shot from a helicopter. On June 10, 2017, while he was working on the sequel of "Beyond Beauty: Taiwan from Above," the helicopter he was riding in crashed into a mountain in Hualien, Taiwan. He died from the crash.

Looking at his BaZi, it is not hard to see that Side Officer was not only present in his BaZi (H3, which was produced by H1) but also in his Grand Fortune (E6) as well as Month Flow (H3) (refer to Figure 49).

These examples show that signs of grave danger can be read from one's BaZi. Mathematically, the probability of all six persons in example A showing signs of being in danger was quite low. As we discussed, such signs do not mean that one is predestined to encounter disasters. It is possible that by taking extra caution and properly "diverting the energy" (see Chapter 8), one can minimize the likelihood and damage of the incoming disaster.

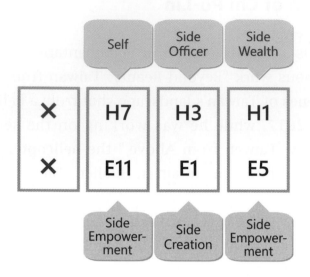

June 2017

| | | |
|---|---|---|
| **Grand Fortune** | E6 | Side Officer |
| **Year Flow** | E10 | Side Peer |
| **Month Flow** | H3 | Side Officer |
| | E7 | Main Officer |

**Figure 49:** BaZi Chart of Mr. Po-Lin Chi

# Case Study 21
# Michael Jordan

(written by my student Shuyu
and proofread by myself)

Michael Jordan was born in Brooklyn, New York, on February 17, 1963, at the hour of E8. He is undeniably among the greatest NBA player is in history. His career has made him into a legend and his fame has lasted that long after his retirement.

In addition to all the championships and personal records he has achieved, what made Jordan's career even more colorful and admirable was that he retired twice at the height of his career, and both times he was able to make a full comeback. His name and reputation have almost become as popular as basketball itself.

Jordan's personal life has also received a lot of public attention. His divorce from his ex-wife, according to the press, made the record of the highest alimony payout. At age 50, he got married again to Yvette Prieto, a Cuban model who was 16 years younger than him.

Jordan's career path and the important events of his life can be seen in his BaZi Chart (Figure 50). Let's take a look together.

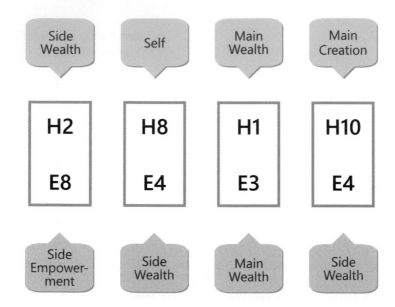

| Side Wealth | Self | Main Wealth | Main Creation |
|---|---|---|---|
| H2<br><br>E8 | H8<br><br>E4 | H1<br><br>E3 | H10<br><br>E4 |
| Side Empowerment | Side Wealth | Main Wealth | Side Wealth |

| Age | 5 | 15 | 25 | 35 | 45 | 55 | 65 | 75 | 85 |
|---|---|---|---|---|---|---|---|---|---|
| Grand Fortune | H10 | H9 | H8 | H7 | H6 | H5 | H4 | H3 | H2 |
| | E2 | E1 | E12 | E11 | E10 | E9 | E8 | E7 | E6 |

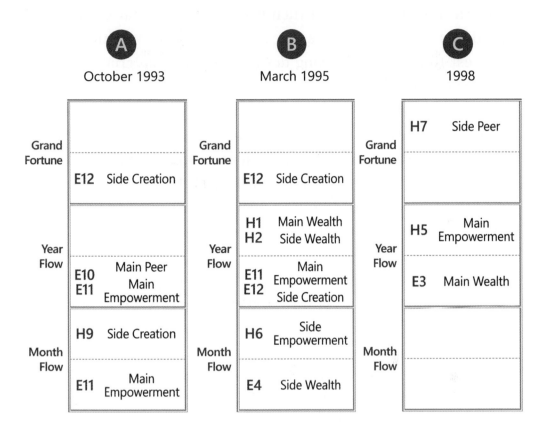

**Figure 50:** BaZi Chart of Michael Jordan

On the Heavenly Stem side, the H1 as Main Wealth sits uninterrupted. The energy is concentrated on H2 as Side Wealth (H8 produces H10 then produces H2). That Creation produces Wealth is obvious. The strong energy of Wealth could suggest that he has a strong desire to pursue material wealth and women. But for an athlete, Wealth can also suggest fame. A strong energy of Wealth could imply his potential to be a star. Also, H8 producing H10 as Main Creation suggests his talent. In his case, it suggests his talent as an athlete.

The Month Branch is Main Wealth. But the two E4 as Side Wealth counter E8 as Side Empowerment. Wealth countering Empowerment suggests that he may not prefer a stable life (as Empowerment represents stability). It could also hint at his propensity to engage in or even be addicted to gambling.

Another important point about his Earthly Branches is that it is very vulnerable against Metal (E9 and E10). Any of these could cause Self countering Wealth. In particular, E10 would cause greater damage since it would be enhanced by E8, and directly counter both E4 on the Earthly Branch. Under such a circumstance, he is not only at risk of losing wealth, but may also encounter problems with his marriage or other relationships.

Jordan because famous very early on his career. His Grand Fortune at age 15 to 25 were H9 and E1; both were Creations. H9 produced H1 as Main Wealth in his BaZi, and E1 produced the two E4 as Side Wealth. The strong Creation producing Wealth allowed him to fully leverage his talent to become rich and famous at a young age.

Then, at age 25, Grand Fortune switched to H8. H8 produced H10 as Main Creation, which in turn produced H2 as Side Wealth. At age 30, Grand Fortune of E12 produced E3 of Main Wealth. The momentum of Creation producing Wealth continued to be strong.

The 20 years (from age 15 to 35) of Creation producing Wealth facilitated Jordan to leverage his talents to its fullest. For an athlete, this is also the most important 20 years of his career.

One major turn of events during this period was his first announcement of retirement in October 1993. In his announcement, he claimed that he had lost his passion for basketball. Some said that his father's death was also a reason. But many speculated that the main reason was the negative publicity surrounding his gambling problem. In March 1995, Jordan announced that he was returning to the Chicago Bulls. Then, he led the team to victory once again.

In October 1993 (year of H10-E10, month of H9-E11), Year Flow contained both E10 and E11, and Month Flow also contained E11 (see Figure 50A). The two E11 of Earth posed strong countering against Grand Fortune of E12, causing Empowerment countering Creation. This could have made him feel depressed. It could also imply that his fame was damaged. At the same time, the E10 on the Year Flow countered the two E4 in his BaZi Chart, constituting Self countering Wealth. E8 in the BaZi Chart produced the E10, making the power of countering stronger. This may have suppressed his desire to pursue material wealth or could have made him less motivated to pursue his career as a basketball player. It could also imply that he had situations where he lost money. Empowerment countering Creation combined with Self Countering Wealth may explain the speculation that he decided to retire because of the negative publicity (damaged fame) he received because of his gambling (countered Wealth) problem.

March 1995 (Year H2-E12, Month H6-E4). Both H2 and E12 of Year Flow started before the year began. H2 was produced by Side Creation H10 in the BaZi. E12 both of Year Flow and Grand Fortune directly produced Main Wealth E3 in the BaZi. Creation producing Wealth showed both on Heavenly Stem and Earthly Branch. As the energy of Wealth was enhanced, so was the will to create wealth. This drove him back on to the basketball court. At the same time, Wealth countering Empowerment also showed on both Heavenly Stem and Earthly Branch. It might have been difficult for him to stay calm and peaceful within (see Figure 50B).

After 20 years of overall good fortune, Grand Fortune switched to H7 from age 35. H7 as Side Peer directly countered Main Wealth H1 in his BaZi. For males, this could either indicate a loss of wealth or problems in the relationship or marriage. Between age 35 and 40, the H7-H1 countering was thorough without any bridging. His relationship with his wife may have taken a turn for the worse during this period. In 2002 (at age 40), his ex-wife Juanita Vanoy asked for a divorce for the first time.

Also, during his Grand Fortune of H7, on January 13, 1999, Jordan announced his second retirement. This announcement also declared the end of the dynasty of the Chicago Bulls. The announcement was before the beginning of Spring and was still in the Year of H5–E3 (see Figure 50C). H5 of Year Flow produced Grand Fortune H7, which further countered H1 in his BaZi, making Peer countering Wealth even more severe. The flow of energy constituted a similar signal as that when he announced his first retirement. Under such a flow of energy, he could easily have lost interest to take on further challenge. And with what he had achieved, there was not much left to feel challenged in NBA.

Jordan's Grand Fortune for the next 20 years (E10, H5, E9, H4) did not make life as easy as the previous 20 years. E9 and E10 countered E3 in his BaZi, forming Peer countering Wealth. H5 countered/coupled with the Side Creation H10. A damaged H10 cannot bridge H8–H2 countering, which was yet another Peer countering Wealth. Moreover, if H7 is present in Year Flow under Grand Fortune of H5, H7 countered Main Wealth H1 in the BaZi. Both H1 and H2 would be damaged.

In Grand Fortune of H4, the flow of production (H8–H10–H2) in the BaZi would enhance H4. The flow of energy concentrates on H4, Side Officer. This could increase the risk of accidents or troubles. Moreover, since in Jordan's BaZi there is no Empowerment on the Heavenly Stem side, he would face countering directly with no protection.

In summary, as we reviewed the BaZi of Michael Jordan, between the ages of 15 and 35 was the period that showed his greatest talents. This was the most important period for an athlete. His talent combined with the facilitation of energy flow from his BaZi and Grand Fortune forged a legendary athlete in the history of the NBA and basketball.

## Case Study 22
## Elizabeth Taylor: the everlasting Cleopatra

Elizabeth Taylor, the legendary Hollywood superstar, started her career in 1942 at the age of 10. She secured her position as one of the most popular actors in Hollywood during the 1950s and1960s. In 1960, she won the Academy Award for Best Actress for the first time with the movie *Butterfield 8*, and again in 1966 with the movie *Who's Afraid of Virginia Woolf?* In addition to her stellar career, her personal life drew a large amount of public attention, especially with her eight marriages and seven husbands.

Through public sources, we find the time of birth of Elizabeth Taylor to be February 27, 1932 at hour of E2 (2:30 a.m. local London local time). Based on Astro Databank (https://www.astro.com/astro-databank), Rodent Rating rated the birth day and time as AA—the most credible. We built her BaZi chart, as shown if Figure 51 (comments: E9 is missing in the chart below).

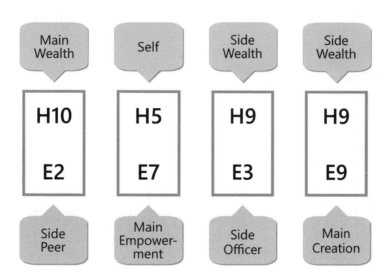

| Age | 8 | 18 | 28 | 38 | 48 | 58 | 68 | 78 | 88 |
|---|---|---|---|---|---|---|---|---|---|
| Grand | H8 | H7 | H6 | H5 | H4 | H3 | H2 | H1 | H10 |
| Fortune | E2 | E1 | E12 | E11 | E10 | E9 | E8 | E7 | E6 |

Grand Fortune switches in year of H1/H6, 9 days after Cold Dew

**Figure 51:** The BaZi Chart of Elizabeth Taylor

The chart, on the Heavenly Stem side, shows coupling of H5-H10, and H5 countering two H9. As both H9 and H10 represent Spirit of Wealth here, it explains her lavish lifestyle and excessive spending. On the Earthly Branch side, Main Creation of E9 signifies her gift for acting and her elegance. The same E9 of Main Creation countering Side Officer of E3 suggests that she was strongly independent, not bound by traditional values. But the countered spirit of Officer also suggests that she had high standards for her other half, who might have found it hard to please her. This also explained why she went through eight marriages.

In Taylor's case, Main Empowerment of E7 on the Earthly branch side suggests that she has a kind and sincere heart. Beginning in the 1980s she devoted herself to charity work. She hosted the first fundraiser for AIDS projects, and later founded the Elizabeth Taylor AIDS Foundation.

Out of curiosity, I analyzed Taylor's Grand Fortune and Year and Month Flow along with the timeline of her marriages, and I found something quite interesting. Taylor always started a marriage when the energy of the Officers rose (H1, H2 or E3, E4, E12). As for her divorces, E9-E3 countering represents Main Creation countering Side Officer. This made it difficult for her to maintain a marriage to begin with. Whenever the energy of Main Creation is enhanced (produced by E5, E11, or reinforced by another E9), Side Officer was further countered, and she usually got divorced during that period.

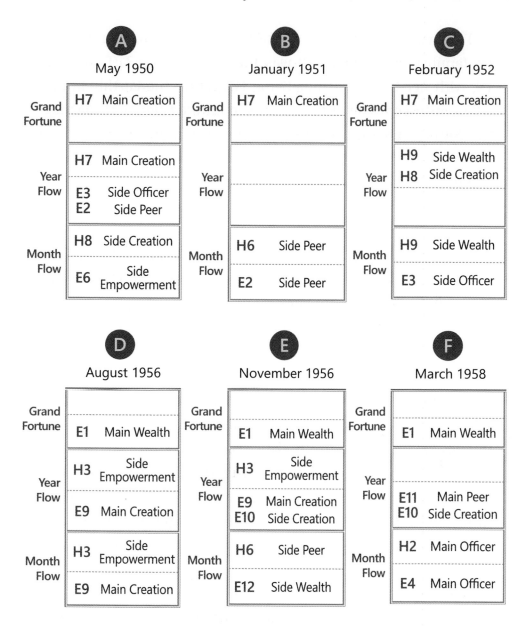

**Figure 52**: Grand Fortune, Year Flow, and Month Flow for Elizabeth Taylor

Taylor's first marriage started on May 6, 1950, and ended on January 29, 1951. 1950 was the year of H7–E3. Taylor was 19, with her Grand Fortune being H7. E3 on the Earthly Branch side reinforced Side Officer, and she entered her first marriage (see Figure 52A). But the energy of E3 only lasted from February 1950 to August 1950. Soon after, her short-lived marriage, which lasted only 268 days, come to an end (see Figure 52B).

Taylor's second marriage started on February 21, 1952, and ended on January 30, 1957. 1952 was the year of H7–E5 and Taylor was still in her Grand Fortune of H7. February, the month of E3, reinforced the energy of her Side Officer (see Figure 52C). She entered her second marriage.

For the year of H7–E5, the energy of E5 started in April and last till October. Such energy could have been detrimental to the marriage. However, Taylor got pregnant likely before this period started, as she gave birth to her first-born son on January 6, 1953. Her pregnancy might have helped maintain her marriage throughout this fragile period. Taylor then gave birth to her second son on February 27, 1955. However, August, 1956 (see Figure 52D), was the year of H3–E9 and month of H8–E2. The energy of E9 emerged in August and lasted till May 1957. That energy of Main Creation again countered her Side Officer of E3. The marriage came to an end in January, 1957.

November 1957 was the month of H6–E12. The energy of E12(W+) as Side Wealth briefly bridged the countering between E9 and E3. This could have had something to do with her third marriage.

Taylor's third marriage was from February 2, 1957, till March 23, 1958. This marriage might have been the result of her pregnancy, as her daughter was born on August 6, 1957. It is reasonable to assume that she got pregnant in November, 1957. As shown in Figure 52E, it was the year of H3–E9 and month of H6–E12. The energy of E9 produces the energy of E12, which then produces that of E3. Side Creation produces Wealth, which then produces Side Officer. The brief surge of energy of Officer brought Taylor a new suitor. In late March 1958, as shown in Figure 52F, she was in Grand Fortune of E1 and it was the year of H5–E11. The energy of H5 was absent during that month. Only the energy of E11 (from October 1957 to April 1958) and E10 was present. The energy of the month was H2–E4. The energy of E11 produced that of E9 (M+), which severely countered Side Officer. Her husband, Mike Todd, died in a plane crash on March 22, 1958.

On one hand, although the countered Side Officer suggested her marriage may not last, on the other hand we found that on the Heavenly Stem side, the energy of H2 as Main officer also came in, plus the energy of E1 produced that of E4 as Main Officer. Could this suggest that she had a new suitor coming along the way?

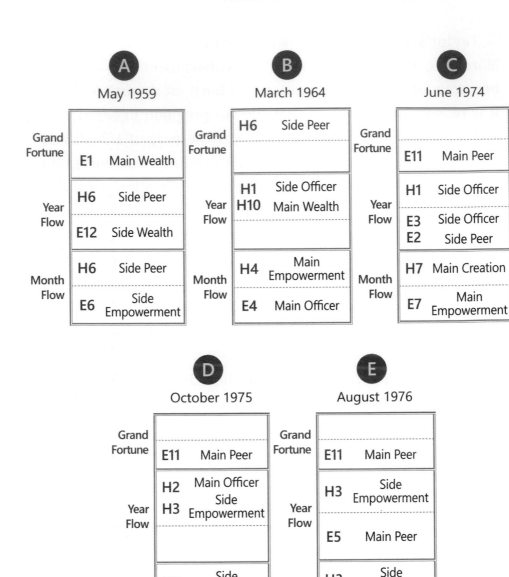

**Figure 53**: Grand Fortune, Year Flow and
Month Flow of Elizabeth Taylor

Taylor's fourth marriage began on May 12, 1959 and ended on March 6, 1964. In May, 1959, as shown in Figure 53A, Taylor was in her Grand Fortune of E1, and the year was H6–E12. The energy of E12 came in between November 1958 and July 1959, and again from November 1959 till July 1960. The energy of E12 can bridge the countering of E11 and E3, but for the year of H5–E11, the energy of E11 (E+) lasted till April of 1959. E11 countered E12, making the bridging ineffective. In May 1959, the energy of E11 subsided, and E12 started to bridge and produce the energy of E3. With the rise of the energy of Officer, Taylor entered her fourth marriage. Taylor divorced her fourth husband, Eddie Fisher, on March 6, 1964, and married Richard Burton. This implied that she had had an affair before her divorce (it was speculated that the affair started during the filming of *Cleopatra* in 1962). In both 1962, year of H9–E3, and 1963, year of H10–E4, Taylor saw the energies of Officers (E3 and E4). In the month of H3–E3 and H4–E4 of 1964, the energy of Officers rose again for Taylor. She fell in love with Richard Burton and divorced her fourth husband Eddie Fisher.

The fifth and sixth marriage were both with Richard Burton, and both ended in divorce. They got married on March 15, 1964, divorced in June 1974, got married again in October 10, 1975, and divorced again on August 1, 1976. In March 1964, as shown in Figure 53B, both the energy of Side Officer of H1 (V+), and Main Officer of E4 (V–) came in. Taylor was married to Richard Burton. In May, her Grand Fortune switched to E12. The energy of E12 (W+) helped bridge the countering of E9 to

E3. She was finally having a smooth and uneventful marriage life throughout those years. The Grand Fortune switched to H5 in May 1969. This does not cause any damage to her relationship, and they were able to maintain their marriage for five more years. In May 1974, however, Grand Fortune switched to E11. Not only her energy of self was raised, but the energy of E11 also intensified the countering of Main Creation to Side Officer. In June, the month of H7–E7, the energy of H7 further countered the energy of H1 of that year (see Figure 53C). Another Main Creation countering Side Officer took place. This ended her ten-year marriage with Richard Burton.

1975 was the year of H2–E4. Both H2 and E4 were Main Officers for Taylor (see Figure 53D). In October, despite the energies of E11 from both Grand Fortune and Month Flow enhancing Main Creation, which countered Side Officer, Taylor still remarried to Richard Burton. This, however, cast a shadow on the marriage. In August 1976 (see Figure 53E), Grand Fortune of E11 plus E5 from the year and E9 from the month further damaged Side Officer. They got divorced yet again.

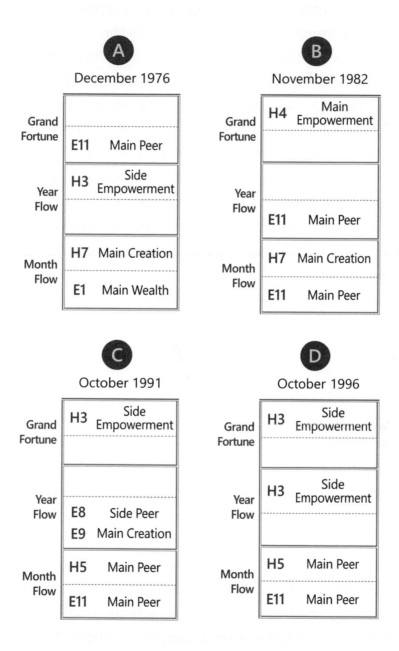

**Figure 54**: Grand Fortune, Year Flow and
Month Flow for Elizabeth Taylor

Taylor's seventh marriage began on December 4, 1976, and ended on November 7, 1982. The year before was H2-E4. Both H2 and E4 were Main Officers for Taylor. This represented a good time to start a new romance. For December 1976, Grand Fortune was E11 with year H3-E5 and month H7-E1 (Figure 54A). Although Grand Fortune of E11 was still against Side Officer, the previous month was H6-E12, and the energy of E12 bridged the countering of Main Creation to Side Officer. In addition, the year of H3 (F+) countered the month of H7 (M+). Empowerment countered Creation. She might not have been thinking through the decision clearly. The marriage lasted till November (month of H7-E11) 1982 (year of H9-E11), as shown in Figure 54B. Her marriage yet again succumbed to the curse of Earth energies (E5 and E11).

One footnote: Some of the sources state that this marriage started on October 4, 1976. When I began the analysis, I used this date and felt that it was a bit odd. It turned out that the date was wrong.

The eighth and the last marriage of Taylor began on October 6, 1991, and ended on October 31, 1996. She was married to Larry Fortensky, a construction worker. As shown in Figure 54C, she was in her Grand Fortune of H3 and year of H8-E8. Fire of H3 produced Earth of H5, which countered Water of H9. H9 as Side Wealth was severely countered. Taylor's role in this marriage, unlike is most marriages, was that of the main supporter of the family. Fortensky a large amount of money and numerous properties from her. On October 31, 1996 (see Figure 54D), the year of H3-E1 and month of H5-E11, E11 again produced E9, which countered Side Officer of E3. She again divorced.

## Case Study 23
## Ernest Hemingway: the Nobel laureate

(Case was written by my student Shuyu
and reviewed by myself)

Ernest Hemingway (1899–1961) was a world-renowned novelist and journalist. He had a profound influence on 20th Century English literature and was hailed as a great novelist. Among his most famous works was, *The Old Man and The Sea,* which won the Pulitzer Prize in 1953. He also won the Nobel Prize for Literature in 1954.

Hemingway was born on July 21, 1899, at the hour of E5 (based on Astro Databank with AA rating) in the suburbs of Chicago, Illinois. As a child, he loved hunting, fishing, and camping. He excelled academically, especially in English. In middle school, he wrote articles for two newspapers. After graduating from high school, he chose to work as a journalist for a newspaper instead of going to college. During World War I, Hemingway volunteered to go to the front line as an ambulance driver. He again went to the front line as a journalist during the Spanish Civil War and World War II. What he saw at the front line later became the material for many of his works. After World War II, he moved to Cuba and focused on writing. Hemingway loved cigarettes and fine wine. He was married four times. His love of hunting and nature lasted throughout his life. Even in his old age he still traveled to remote locations. His journeys to the front lines as well as into the wilderness left some wounds and diseases. After he moved back to the United States, he was constantly troubled by his wound and by depression. Eventually, he killed himself in his home. A tough man like him who went to so many battlefields and wrote so many inspirational works, and who eventually chose to take his own life, shocked many people. Here we try to understand his life and his mind from the perspective of BaZi.

H6 produces H8 forming Empowerment producing Peer (see Figure 55). This implies that he had received help throughout his life and was able to make a living easily. The Main Creation producing Side Wealth (E12 producing E3) represents that he was able to create wealth with his own talents. The strong energy of Side Wealth also revealed his love of enjoying cigarette and wine, his interest of traveling around the world, as well as his colorful history of romance and marriage.

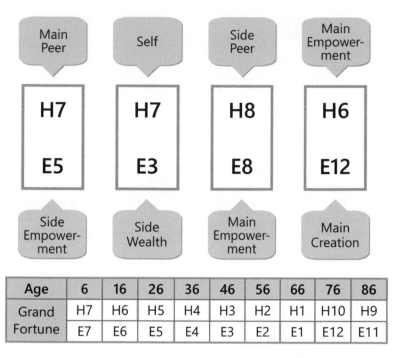

| Age | 6 | 16 | 26 | 36 | 46 | 56 | 66 | 76 | 86 |
|---|---|---|---|---|---|---|---|---|---|
| Grand | H7 | H6 | H5 | H4 | H3 | H2 | H1 | H10 | H9 |
| Fortune | E7 | E6 | E5 | E4 | E3 | E2 | E1 | E12 | E11 |

**Figure 55:** BaZi Chart of Ernest Hemingway

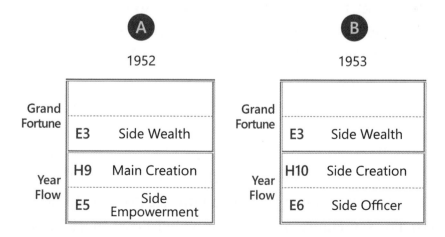

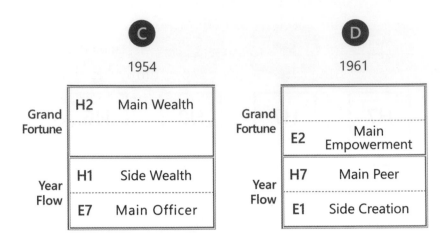

**Figure 56:** Grand Fortune, Year and Month Flow
of Hemingway during different years

On the flip side, Side Wealth countering Side Empowerment (E3 countering E5) makes him mentally unsettled. Empowerment represents stability. A person with countered Empowerment is prone to move or travel a lot. Hemingway started to travel around the world in his early years and lived in Cuba for some years.

In 1952, he published *The Old Man and The Sea* (see Figure 56A). H9 in Year Flow represented his Main Creation. The two H7 in his BaZi, combined with H6 producing H8, resulted in strong energy of the Peers, which enhanced Main Creation. With this novel, Hemingway won a Pulitzer Prize in 1953 (Year of H10-E6, see Figure 56B), and a Nobel Prize in 1954 (Year of H1-E7, see Figure 56C). He was under Grand Fortune of E3.

In 1953, E3 produced the E6 of the Year Flow, and E6 then produced E5 in his BaZi. This constituted Officer producing Empowerment. In 1954, E7 of Year Flow produced E8 in the BaZi, again forming Officer producing Empowerment. With the strong flow of energy in two consecutive years, it is not surprising that he was recognized with such prestigious honors.

Unfortunately, in his last years, Hemingway was troubled by his physical and mental conditions and eventually took his own life in 1961 (see Figure 56D). He attempted suicide in the previous spring (1960, Year of H7-E1). At that time, he was under Grand Fortune of E2. E2 coupled with E1 of Grand Fortune, causing Empowerment countering Creation, a common sign of depression.

Coincidentally, the energy of E1 started in December 1959 and lasted till July 1960, and then resumed from December 1960 to July 1961. Hemingway killed himself in July 1961, exactly the last month of the energy of E1. One could not help but wonder if things would have turned out differently if he could have just hung on and made it through the month.

# Case Study 24
# Starry Starry Night: the life of Vincent Van Gogh

Upon first looking at the BaZi of Vincent Van Gogh (March 30, 1853–July 29, 1890. BaZi chart shown in Figure 57), one may wonder if it is even correct. How could a great artist such as Van Gogh not have a BaZi with a concentrated energy of Creation? As we have learned, the energy of Creation represents one's intellect and talent for art. This would seem very odd. But once we study in detail the life of Van Gogh and his corresponding Grand Fortune, Year Flow, and Month Flow, we find that everything fits just right. The energy of Grand Fortune, Year Flow, and Month Flow can influence one's life in fundamental ways.

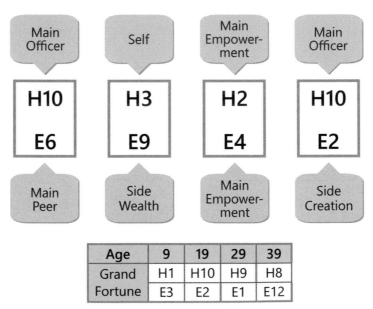

| Age | 9 | 19 | 29 | 39 |
|---|---|---|---|---|
| Grand | H1 | H10 | H9 | H8 |
| Fortune | E3 | E2 | E1 | E12 |

**Figure 57:** BaZi Chart of Vincent Van Gogh

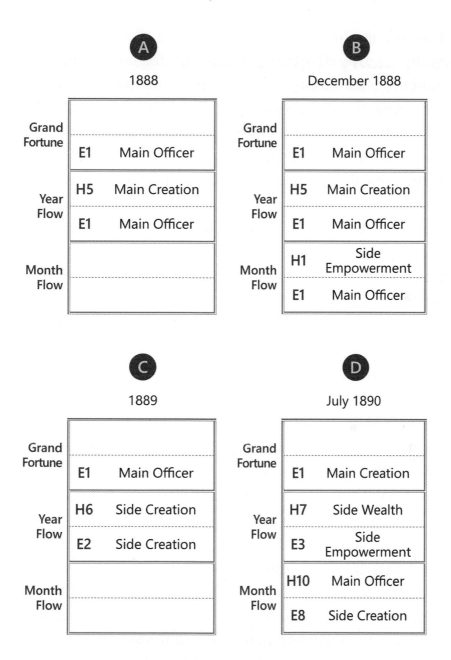

**Figure 58:** Grand Fortune, Year Flow, and Month Flow for Van Gogh

Looking at the BaZi of Van Gogh, on the Heavenly Stem side he has two H10 that produce H2, forming Main Officer producing Main Empowerment. This indicates that he had a noble character and a kind and good personality. Influenced by his father who was a church minister, he was committed to his religion and started preaching when he was 23 years old. He dedicated himself to studying the Bible for five years and was determined to spread the gospel and help the poor. His pure, noble, and unselfish personality reflects the strong energy of Empowerment.

The energy of Empowerment can also be seen in the way that he was taken good care of by his "Noble Person"—his brother Theo. Theo not only helped Vincent financially but also gave him vital mental support in times of need. This made it possible for him to focus on painting.

On the Earthly Branch side, however, E4 countering E2 represents Main Empowerment countering Side Creation. This explains why Van Gogh suffered from depression throughout his life. The E6–E9 coupling transformed E6 into E12. E12 is Side Officer, which pressured him into painting diligently, creating works of art one after another. But since there is no Creation producing Wealth in his BaZi, he did not have much luck financially. Throughout his life, he only sold two of his paintings.

Vincent Van Gogh and his brother Theo were very close. He wrote more than 650 letters to Theo. In those letters, he talked about his ideas, plans, and expectations for his painting, as well as his self-reflection. All these letters have been well kept to today. They help us understand his state of mind when he was creating his masterpieces.

On Van Gogh's Earthly Branch side, there is an E4 countering E2, which maps to Main Empowerment countering Side Creation. This is bad for the creator. It suppresses one's creativity as well as the drive to create. However, his Grand Fortune switched to E2 as Side Creation at the age of 24 (nominal age). And for four consecutive years—25 (year of H4-E2), 26 (year of H5-E3), 27 (year of H6-E4), and 28 (year of H6-E5)—the energy of Creation was present (E2, H5, H6, E5). The energy of Creation accumulated inside him and finally erupted. In 1880, at the age of 28, he discontinued his priesthood and decided to focus on painting. For an artist, this was quite a late start. In the next ten years, he was devoted to the goal he set up. "The only choices I have are, to be a good painter, or to be a bad one." He said. Van Gogh was a pilgrim with regards to the artistic path that he set out for himself. His faith in the art was unswerving. In his letter to Theo, he wrote: "I have found something that I can put my mind and soul in. I feel encouraged and have discovered the meaning of my life."

At age 29, Van Gogh's Grand Fortune switched to H9 as Side Officer. The energy of Side Office drove Van Gogh to putting all his efforts into his work. There was no H1 or H5 to mitigate the pressure from Side Officer. The stress brought by Side Officer directly influenced him, gradually pushing him to the edge of a breakdown. Moreover, Main Empowerment countering Side Creation (E4 countering E2) compounded the stress with depression.

1888 (year of H5–E1, age 36) and 1889 (year of H6–E2, age 37), were two of the most critical years for Van Gogh (see Figures 58A and C). Not only was he most productive, but it was also during this period that he created most of his representative works. However, it was also the same period that he suffered the most from his mental illness. His mood swung from the valley of depression to the height of mania. He was even admitted to a mental hospital a few times as a result of having nervous breakdowns. In the year of H5–E1, he was under Grand Fortune of E1 (Main Officer). In August, he moved to Arles, in southern France, so that he could focus on painting. Under the catalyst of H5 as Main Creation, he was full of energy and inspiration to create. He even invited Gauguin to live with him. However, the E1 in both his Grand Fortune and Year Flow also enhanced the E4–E2 countering, making Empowerment countering Creation more severe. This was reflected in his deteriorating mental condition and his disagreements with and confrontation against Gauguin. In December (Month of E1), after a serious confrontation with Gauguin, Van Gogh cut his left ear with a razor. As shown in Figure 58B, during that month he had H1 countering H5 on the Heavenly Stem, plus three E1 that enhanced E4, which countered E2. The situation of Empowerment countering Creation reached a new height. Before he committed suicide on July 27, 1890, he had four major episodes of mental breakdown. All of them happened during the months of E1, E2, and E8. He said "I feel so sad and distressed. Words cannot describe the way I feel. It was like I am drowning in the ocean."

In 1889 (Year of H6-E2), the two H10 produced H2, which countered H6 in Year Flow, forming Main Empowerment countering Side Creation. Also, the E2 of Year Flow countered the E1 of Grand Fortune, forming Side Creation countering Main Officer. Van Gogh's mental condition swung between depression and mania. When his condition was less severe, he asked his doctor to let him paint, and he would keep painting with no rest and no sleep, letting the frenzy built up inside him until he collapsed and had to stop and be treated. He even changed his style of painting. He said, "Every technique I learned in Paris was gone. I had returned to the state I was at home before I knew the impressionists." "I want to paint it so simply that everyone can understand immediately." During his stay in the hospital in Arles, he produced more than 200 paintings, including *The Starry Night*, *Café de Nuit,* and *The Sunflowers.*

In July 1890 (see Figure 58D), Van Gogh finished his work *Wheatfield with Crow*. The feeling of unsettledness in the painting seemed to imply that this was his last outcry. He wrote to Theo that he had made a point of expressing sadness, later adding "extreme loneliness." The swirl of depression was about to swallow him. He had consumed his last drop of passion and love of life. Two weeks later, he shot himself in the chest with a pistol, leaving behind works of art that he burnt his life creating.

## Case Study 25
## The 2016 US presidential election:
## Donald Trump vs. Hillary Clinton

The 2016 presidential election in the United States was among the most dramatic and unpredictable in the country's history. Donald Trump, who announced his intention to run, won the nomination in July 2016 and defeated his Democratic opponent, Hillary Clinton, a veteran in Washington DC and the first female presidential candidate in US history. Although Clinton won more popular votes, Trump won more electoral votes and won the presidential campaign.

Based on Astro Databank (www.astro.com/astro-databank), Trump's date and time of birth is June 14, 1946, at 10:54 a.m. The website rated his birth date and time as AA, which is the most credible. With this, we can plot Trump's BaZi, as shown in Figure 59. Note that the H1 in his Month Pillar is transformed into H5 as a result of H1–H6 coupling.

The first thing we notice is that among the eight elements, H3, E6 are Main Empowerment and H7 are Side Empowerment. This shows the energy of Empowerment is strong. It is very common that those with strong energy of Empowerment have strong interests in real estate or investment. For Trump, this is the case.

Other than the energy of Empowerment, his energy of Self is even stronger, with two H6 on the Heavenly Stem, E8, and E11 on the Earthly Branch, plus the transformed H1. Among the eight elements, he has five elements of Self, which are further enhanced by the elements of Empowerment. People with such strong energy of Self would have very high self-confidence (maybe over-confidence in some cases). They pay less attention to the opinions of others and are less likely to be easily influenced. Sometimes they could be seen as egocentric.

In April 2014, Trump's Grand Fortune switched to H8. The two H6 in his BaZi enhanced H8 as Main Creation, facilitating the rise of his fame. In 2015 Year Flow switched to H2-E8. H8 countering H2 is Creation countering Officer. He could not care less about any rules or conventional wisdom and decided to run for president.

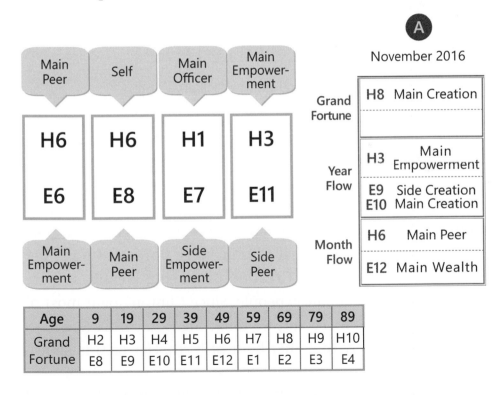

| Age | 9 | 19 | 29 | 39 | 49 | 59 | 69 | 79 | 89 |
|---|---|---|---|---|---|---|---|---|---|
| Grand | H2 | H3 | H4 | H5 | H6 | H7 | H8 | H9 | H10 |
| Fortune | E8 | E9 | E10 | E11 | E12 | E1 | E2 | E3 | E4 |

**Figure 59:** BaZi Chart of Donald Trump

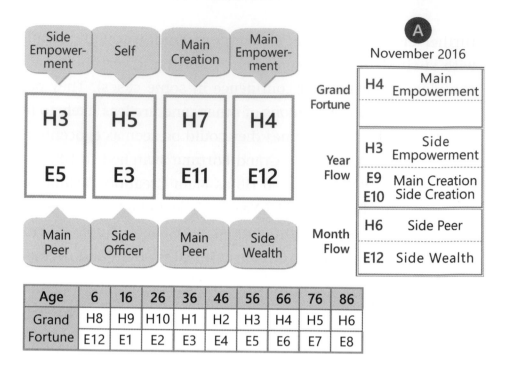

**Figure 60:** BaZi Chart of Hillary Clinton

The birth date of Hillary Clinton is October 26, 1947. Her time of birth was not confirmed. Astro Databank shows that her time of birth was 8:14 a.m., but the website also rated the birth time as DD (not very credible). Different sources also show different times. Some say 8 a.m. and others say 8 p.m. From a BaZi perspective, if Clinton were born at 8 p.m., her BaZi would show strong Creation producing Wealth, a more common trait for business people. Since Clinton spent most of her life in the public sector, we think the Hour of E5 (7 a.m.–9 a.m.) is more likely to be her hour of birth. Her BaZi is shown in Figure 60.

Between the ages of 36 and 56, she was under Grand Fortune of Officers (H1, E3, H2, E4) for 20 consecutive years.

This fit her career path. In her BaZi, H3 produces H5, which then produces H7. The energy concentrated on H7 as Main Creation, signaling that she is an intelligent and eloquent person. Also, the energy on the Earthly Branch concentrates on E3 as Side Officer. This implies that she is a highly determined person with a strong drive to get things done.

In 1974, Clinton participated in the Watergate investigation on President Nixon. This started her career in politics. Year Flow in 1974 was H1–E3. H1 produced H3 in her BaZi, forming Officer producing Empowerment. The following year (Year of H2-E4), H2 again formed Officer producing Empowerment with H4 in her BaZi. For those who pursue a career in public service, this was good fortune. In 2014 and 2015, Year Flow again switched to H1 and H2. Her fortune turned strong again. With that, she won the Democrat nomination to run for president.

The date of the election was November 8, 2016. Fortune for both candidates in that month are shown in Figures 59A and 60A. Both candidates have Earth element as Self, so the Year Flow and Month Flow posed Creation producing Wealth for them both. But as Trump had strong energy concentrated on E11 of his BaZi (E11 produced the E9 in Year Flow, which then produced E12 of the Month Flow, forming a perfect flow of energy), Clinton, on the other hand, had E9 producing E12 in her BaZi. E12 then produced E3. Enhanced E3 as Side Officer made it more likely for her to be framed, blackmailed, or backstabbed. Just within two weeks before the election, the FBI director announced that they would reopen the investigation of Clinton's emails. This news caused great damage to her campaign.

As for Trump, H8 of his Grand Fortune coupled with H3 in his BaZi. This also formed Empowerment countering Creation. The two H6 helped bridge the situation, so this countering was not severe. But people under the condition of Empowerment countering Creation tend to make inappropriate comments, which could be fatal during a presidential election (indeed, Trump made some controversial comments during his campaign). To Trump's favor, Month Flow switched to H6–E12 from early November. H6 of Month Flow diffused the countering.

Overall, from a BaZi perspective, the election was a close match. Both sides were under strong fortune but with some risk factors. Trump had the risk of making wrong comments, while Clinton had the risk of backstabbing or litigation. But the situation in early November was slightly in favor of Trump. If the election date were moved to some other time, the result might have been different.

## Case Study 26
## 2017 French presidential election: Macron vs. Le Pen

The 2017 French Presidential Election was held in two rounds—the first round on April 23 and the second round on May 7. In the first round, Emmanuel Macron from En Marche! (EM) and Marine Le Pen from National Front (FN) got most of the votes (23% and 21% respectively). As no candidate won over

50% of the vote, the second round was held on May 7. Macron defeated Le Pen with 66.06% of the votes and became the 25th President of France.

The birth date and time of both candidates are recorded in Astro Databank with the highest credibility ratings (AA). Macron was born on December 21, 1977, at 10:40 a.m. (Hour of E6). Le Pen was born on August 5, 1968, at 11:20 a.m. (Hour of E7).

Figures 61 and 62 shows the BaZi charts of both candidates. Macron has Creation producing Wealth in the Heavenly Stem side. Le Pen has four elements of Creation in his BaZi. Both show signs of being creative, charismatic, and able to rally supporters. In the first round of the election on April 23, Macron showed Officer producing Empowerment in his Earthly Branch, and Le Pen showed Creation producing Wealth in her Earthly Branch. Both were under good fortune. On the Heavenly Stem side, Macron showed signs of Creation countering Officer, and Le Pen had slight Empowerment countering Creation. All in all, they were quite equally matched as far as their BaZi goes during the first round.

Month Flow switched to H2–E6 on April 27. On May 7, the day of the second round election, the energy of H2 dominated the Month Flow, but the energy of E6 is also present. For Macron, H2 produced H4, forming a good fortune of Creation producing Wealth. E6 did not damage his Wealth. For Le Pen, however, E6 created Peer countering Wealth. The two E8 in his BaZi are yin Earth and could not provide much help. Macron widened the gap over Le Pen and won the election with flying colors.

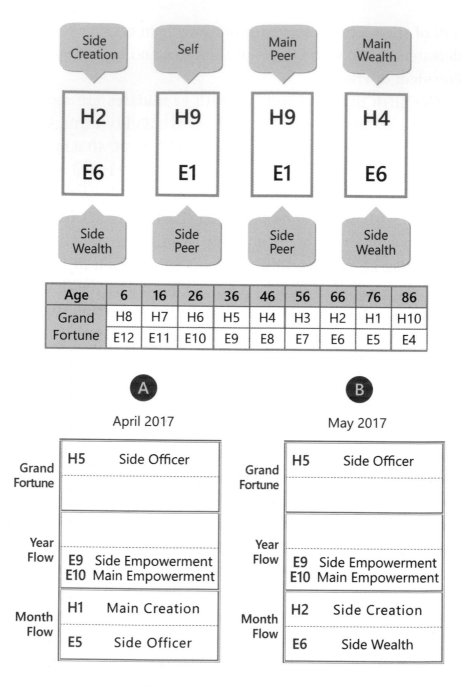

**Figure 61:** BaZi Chart of Macron

The Science of BaZi Analysis: Grand Fortune, Year Flow, and Month Flow

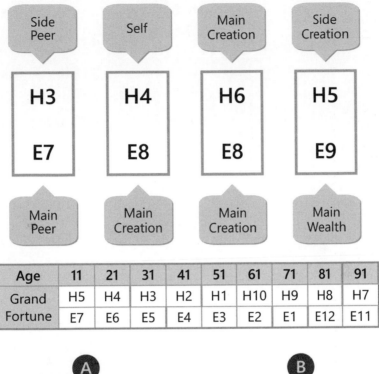

| Age | 11 | 21 | 31 | 41 | 51 | 61 | 71 | 81 | 91 |
|---|---|---|---|---|---|---|---|---|---|
| Grand Fortune | H5 | H4 | H3 | H2 | H1 | H10 | H9 | H8 | H7 |
| | E7 | E6 | E5 | E4 | E3 | E2 | E1 | E12 | E11 |

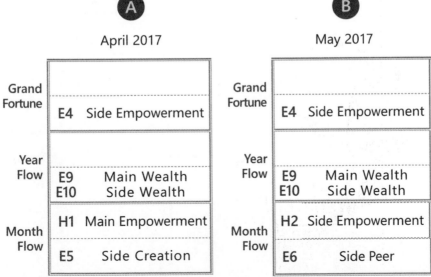

**Figure 62:** BaZi Chart of Le Pen

# Chapter 6

# Taking Your BaZi
# Analysis Skills to
# the Next Level

Once we are familiar with all the basics and are sufficiently confident with the case examples in the last chapter, we may wish to hone our skills further so we can help others. Some say that to become a professional BaZi practitioner, one has to study at least ten years. In my opinion, without the right method and system, the ten years would just be a waste of time.

For example, there is a very commonly used BaZi analytical framework which divides people into three classes—the "Bodily Strong," the "Bodily Weak," and the "Bodily Balanced." Based on the classification, the framework then decides the "favored Spirits" among the Ten Spirits, and then determines if the luck is in favor of the person based on the number of favored Spirits shown in Grand Fortune, Year Flow, and Month Flow.

If we apply this framework to Case Study 7 of Chapter 5 (The Life of Echo), the BaZi of Echo is undoubtedly Bodily Weak, and the framework would tell us that Peer and Empowerment would be her favored Spirits, and she would have been in good fortune when these spirits were present. However, we have seen time and again in her case, Empowerment proved to be extremely bad luck for her.

I have also seen first hand people making wrong decisions based on this framework. One of them mistakenly believed that he was under good fortune and aggressively invested in the stock market with his pension, and another decided to run for an election. Both ended up with catastrophic failure. My experience tells me that studying them does not help much. This is why I do not believe in any traditional BaZi framework that does not conform to the basic principles of yin-yang and the Five Elements.

So in my opinion, staying in the correct direction with the right concept is far more important than studying all the books of BaZi. It is essential to master the interactions among the Five Elements, as well as the dynamics between one's BaZi and Grand Fortune, Year Flow, and Month Flow. Readers who can understand the case examples in Chapter 5 with ease should already possess basic BaZi skills. It took me years of self-study and research to get to this level. Readers who study this book carefully should be able to achieve this within a few months.

Once the basic skills are there, the next step is to apply them to real cases. A good practitioner should be able to confidently apply his or her skills to all cases presented. But how do we get there?

My suggestion is to start with people you know best. Try to build BaZi charts for your family and close friends. Verify their personalities and the events that happened to them and match that against their BaZi. In my experience, such exercise can be very frustrating at first, as we are likely to be unable to find any correlation between the person's life or personality and his or her BaZi, and it could take us a lot of time to run the analysis. But do not despair. The inconsistency is most likely due to an incomplete analysis and failure to cover all the dynamics among the Five Elements. As we get more proficient, we should be able to see a match or pattern and run the analysis faster. Performing BaZi analysis is, in a way, like solving a math problem. Even though one has studied the theory, it still takes practice to solve math problems quickly and proficiently.

With sufficient practice, one should get better and more accurate. But don't be too hard on yourself if you miss something. No one can be 100 percent accurate all the time, myself included. But years of practice and feedback from my clients have helped me improve. With each feedback I received after every error I made, it would be very hard for me to be wrong again when I see the same pattern.

One additional point. A BaZi practitioner is also subject to his or her fortune of BaZi. When the practitioner is under the influence of Empowerment countering Creation, the chance of making a mistake could be a lot higher. But to think about it, most good practitioners are strong with the energy of Creation and Empowerment. Energy of Creation brings good analytical skills while the energy of Empowerment makes one interested in subjects of life and fortune. It takes both to be a good BaZi practitioner. But this also means that Empowerment countering Creation is likely to happen at some point in time. What kind of BaZi charts could have both the power of Empowerment and Creation without serious countering between them? Those who are interested could think about this.

Some BaZi instructors like to have their students practice with the BaZi of celebrities. Indeed, nowadays it is easy to find birth dates and times of many celebrities over the Internet, and this book uses case studies of celebrities in some of the examples. Still, I recommend that we start with people we know intimately. After all, you know the lives of these persons the best and will be able to verify if your analysis is correct. The stories of celebrities are not always true and complete, and their birth dates and time may not always be accurate. When I was studying BaZi and trying to develop my system of analysis, I had spent years observing the flow of fortune of my own family members and close friends and made sure that my analysis could sufficiently explain everything before I was confident to release my system to the public. Since our readers have the benefit of studying my system instead of having to develop one from scratch, in most cases, it should take months instead of years to be sufficiently proficient.

One important note. One should be very sensitive and careful when reading and informing the fortune of your practice subjects, especially before one is confident or proficient with his or her skill. Also, using the information from the analysis to manipulate others is highly unethical and should not be done under any circumstances.

# Section 1
# The influence of Month Flow

In Section 1 of Chapter 5, we illustrated the beginning and end of the energy of Year Flow. Readers who studied Chapter 5 in detail should have realized that, without getting the timing of the energy of Year Flow right, it is impossible to make an accurate analysis.

In fact, the timing of Month Flow also matters, and it does not start right at the change of each solar term. For example, the month of H10-E4 in 2012 started on the day of Waking of Insects. But the energy of H10 and E4 did not start exactly on that day.

Some books say that the energy of H10 covered the first half of month while the energy of E4 covered the second half. This is quite close, but from my study I concluded that the following rules are more accurate:

## Rule 1

The energy of Month Flow on the Heavenly Stem starts before the month starts. It starts from the day with the same Heavenly Stem before the beginning of the month and remains strong till the next Day with the same Heavenly Stem; then it is weakened but still present until the next solar term. If the Heavenly Stem is with yin attributes, then energy starts a day earlier (on the day of the same element with yang attributes).

For example, in 2012, the month of H2-E6 started on the May 5 (beginning of Summer). The energy of H2 of Month Flow started from the closest day of H1 before May 5. This was May 3, the day of H1-E1. The energy of H2 lasted till May 14, the day of H2-E12 and subsequently turned weak.

Why did the energy start on the day of H1-E1 (May 3) instead of H2-E2 (May 4)? I think this is probably because the energy can be induced by the energy of the same element, regardless of yin and yang.

## Rule 2

The energy of Month Flow on the Earthly Branch side starts weak and turns strong after the energy of Heavenly Stem turns weak and on the day of the same Earthly Branch.

Using the same example, the energy of H2 faded on May 14 (day of H2-E6). The next closest day of E6 was on May 20 (day of H8-E6). The energy of E6 of Month Flow was enhanced on that day.

Note that while the rules help decide the periods when the energies are strong, the energies of Month Flow are present throughout the month. When the energy of Heavenly Stem is strong, the energy of Earthly Branch, although weak, is not absent. In practice, here are a couple of suggestions:

1. In general, if we read any sign that is caused by Month Flow, we should remind the client to pay attention five to 10 days before the beginning of the month. For the signs that could imply serious consequences, we should ask the client to pay attention throughout the entire month even though the energy does not remain strong all the time.

2. Simply dividing the energy of Heavenly Stem and Earthly Branch into the first and second half of the month, although not 100 percent accurate, is still in general correct. If we do not have a perpetual calendar to look up when we conduct the analysis, we could simply analyze as such.

# Section 2
# How to analyze one's wealth

For anyone who practices any form of fortune-telling in any part of the world, money is probably the most often asked topic. All of us hope to be better off economically, and most of my clients would like to know when they will have opportunities to make money.

When my BaZi analytical system first took shape, and I started to practice with it, there was a time when I did not notice any signs of money making events in my analysis. This bothered me a lot, to the extent that for a while I was hesitant to take any clients.

After spending more reviewing the cases, I realized that in BaZi there are two types of signs of gaining wealth. One type is through the person's talents and efforts. This is symbolized by Creation producing Wealth. In this case, Main Wealth symbolizes Wealth made through a stable or normal method (e.g., a good job), while Side Wealth symbolizes that Wealth is made with a more risky way (e.g., risky investment), but the amount could also be larger.

The second type of wealth is more passive. For example, wealth gained through inheritance, pension, gift, easy jobs or lifetime employment (government jobs in some countries for example). This is usually symbolized by Officer producing Empowerment. In some cases, we see people around us who do not work very hard or have any special skills but are still taken good care of by people from the top at the workplace, or by senior members of the family.

In summary, those who have Creation producing Wealth should make the best use of it and strive to create wealth with his or her own ideas and efforts. This could be starting one's own business, managing personal investments, taking on extra jobs, and so on. On the other hand, those who are strong with Officer producing Empowerment are more suitable for working in large corporations or the government.

# Section 3
# Special BaZi patterns

Once a while, we encounter people with very special BaZi patterns. Among these patterns, two are worthy of discussion. In traditional BaZi terminology, they are called "submissive patterns" (*cong shi ge* 從勢格) and "full dominative pattern" (*zhuan wang ge* 專旺格). All other BaZi patterns are called "regular pattern" (*zheng ge* 正格). All examples and case studies up to this point belong to regular pattern. Submissive pattern and dominative pattern are not common. Not many people I know have such patterns. But I did encounter a few in my practice.

## Submissive Pattern

The BaZi chart of a submissive pattern contains no Empowerment nor Peer (except for Self). In other words, all the seven elements other than Self are Wealth, Officer, or Creation. Figure 63 shows an example.

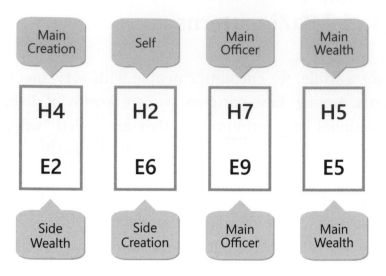

**Figure 63:** The BaZi Chart of a submissive pattern

Many books discuss the submissive pattern. The definition in each book may be slightly different. The main difference is around whether the submissive pattern is strictly defined as above, or whether the BaZi charts with one Peer or Empowerment other than Self can also be considered as submissive pattern.

Why does this pattern matter for traditional BaZi practitioners? In short, it matters because traditional BaZi practitioners do not follow the same logic of analysis as we do, and the BaZi charts of submissive pattern, under their way of analysis, the predicted events would come out wrong or entirely opposite to what they say. So they must treat this as an exceptional case. In the traditional BaZi analytical method, a chart must first be classified under a few categories such as strong/weak (*wang/ruo* 旺弱) and dominative/submissive (*zhuan/cong* 專從), then using these metrics to decide its preference/taboo (*xi/ji* 喜忌) and the fortunes. Based on this framework, the BaZi charts of the submissive pattern are considered extremely weak, and it would be the best if it were enhanced by the energy of Empowerment and Peer to achieve balance.

But in this practice, traditional practitioners noticed that things could be quite the opposite. Many people with a submissive pattern often have bad fortune under the energy of Empowerment and Peer. So they conclude that the submissive pattern should be treated as an exception, in which they favor the energies of Wealth, Officer and Creation.

In modern scientific research, a good theory should be able to explain all scenarios. If a theory has major exceptions, it is either incorrect or incomplete. In our BaZi analytical system, we analyze those with submissive patterns in the same way as we analyze the regular ones. There is no need to divide the charts into strong or weak as we analyze them just the same.

Let's revisit the submissive pattern with what we have learned. If a chart contains Creation, Officer, and Wealth evenly, they are not that different from a regular chart. On the other hand, if a chart contains mostly Wealth, the presence of Peer would cause serious damage (Peer Countering Wealth), while the presence of Creation would be a good sign (Creation Producing Wealth).

Furthermore, if a chart contains lots of Creation, the presence of Empowerment would cause a serious threat of Empowerment countering Creation. This is exactly what we saw in the case of Echo in Chapter 5. On the contrary, a chart with lots of Officers would love to see the presence of Empowerment, and would contradict the framework of submissive pattern as predicted by traditional BaZi theories.

As such, we can see that it is neither effective nor accurate to force all BaZi charts into a few patterns. Doing so would only create exceptions that require more special rules to cover, and in turn, create even more exceptions. All we need to do is go back to the basic principles, and we should be able to cover all the cases.

## Dominative Pattern

The other special pattern is called dominative pattern. A BaZi chart of a dominative pattern includes only Peer and Empowerment. Most books would say that Month Branch has to be Peer to qualify as dominative pattern. An example of this pattern is shown in Figure 64.

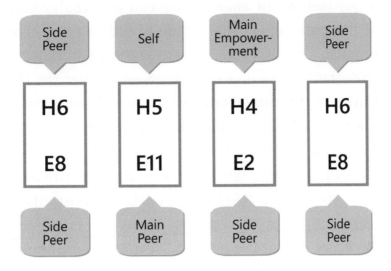

**Figure 64:** The BaZi chart of a dominative pattern

A few famous persons have BaZi charts of dominative pattern. The scientist Richard Feynman (1918-1988) is one example. I don't have many cases of such patterns from my practice.

According to traditional BaZi theories, those with dominative pattern see the presence of Peer or Empowerment as good fortune. Just like the submissive pattern, to them, this pattern is also an exceptional case. The reason is that according to traditional BaZi theory, those with too many Peer and Empowerment are too strong in their Self, and should be balanced with Wealth, Officer, or Creation. For those with dominative pattern, this is not the case, and traditional BaZi theory has to treat it as another exceptional case.

With our method of analysis, we can just analyze any BaZi chart of this pattern as usual. There would be no difference in our approach. The only thing that is worth mentioning is that, if the BaZi chart is dominative pattern and either the Heavenly Stem or the Earthly Branch has no Empowerment, it would be very vulnerable in front of the energy of Officer, as the energy Officer would directly counter the Peers.

In the example of Figure 64, the Empowerment on the Heavenly Stem side (H4) will create Officer producing Empowerment when the energy of Officer is present. But since the Peers are on the outside (Year Stem and Hour Stem), they would first interact with the energy of Officer before the Empowerment of H4. Some Officer countering Peer may still occur before Officer producing Empowerment.

On the Earthly Branch side, however, all the Peers are unprotected. In the presence of strong energy of Officer, the person is not likely to have a good fortune.

As we discussed in Section 2 of this chapter, both Wealth and Empowerment can be signs of making money. Since someone with the BaZi chart of dominative pattern does not have Wealth, their fortune with money is analyzed based on their Empowerment. They usually have good fortune in the presence of Empowerment and have a tough time when Empowerment is countered or coupled.

As for the energy of Wealth, it is usually not easy for people with dominative pattern to make money when Wealth is present. In their BaZi chart, the energy of Peer is almost certain to be strong, so most of the time the presence of Wealth is countered by Peer. The only exception is with the presence of Creation as the bridge, but this at best temporary.

Peer countering Wealth can also manifest in personal relationships. For males with dominative pattern, the countering may manifest on his wife or father. I have one male client who has BaZi chart of dominative pattern. He is tall, handsome, graduated from the top college, and is the top executive of a high-tech company. With all the best qualifications one can get, he is still single with no girlfriend (and no, he is not a gay).

Those of dominative pattern and have Empowerment both on Heavenly Stem and Earthly Branch, especially on the Year and Hour pillars, are relatively immune from backstabbing. Moreover, the presence of Officer brings them the perfect opportunity for promotion or rise to power.

To close this section, if you look up books on traditional BaZi theories, you will find a lot of patterns other than these two, along with many different cases that require different treatments. In my opinion, however, this only implies that the theory is not sound. I believe that as long as we stick to the principle of the Five Elements, we can analyze any case.

# Section 4
# When hour of birth is uncertain

In our method of analysis, the elements of the four pillars—year, month, day, and hour—are equally important. Missing any single element could lead to very different results. For most persons, the year, month and date of birth can hardly be mistaken. Hour of birth, however, is often uncertain or inaccurate. It is very important to get the hour of birth right before we analyze BaZi.

In Section 4 of Chapter 4, we mentioned that the time of birth should be the moment when the baby comes in contact with the surrounding air (in Chinese we use the word *qi* "氣"). In many cases, it takes some time after a baby's head first comes into contact with the air and until the doctor finish the delivery. So the birth time on the hospital record may be a bit late. If we find that the BaZi does not match the client, we could try to move the hour ahead by one pillar.

There are also cases when the client does not know his own time of birth. I had a client whose father and mother could not agree on his hour of birth. How would we analyze such a case? Some ancient books talk about using certain body features such as the number and direction of hair swirls. But these methods are neither proven nor used by many. Instead, here are a few methods that I use:

1. By the look of their eyes: each time I shared this with my friends, they thought I was either insane or had some supernatural sixth sense. In fact, this is merely a skill built upon years of face-to-face consulting practice. I believe anyone with my experience could do it. Usually, a person with a strong energy of Creation has a certain spark in their eyes. Someone with strong energy of Empowerment has a more benevolent look, speaks slowly, and displays little movement.

2. By the character of the person

3. By the physical conditions and history of diseases

4. Based on major events that happened in his or her life. For example, the years when major countering occur (especially from the Officers)

Here is one example. Figures 65 and 66 are two possible BaZi charts of a gentleman born in May 1945. He was not sure whether he was born at the hour of E5 or E4, as Taiwan was practicing Daylight Saving Time during that period.

From the beginning of our counseling session, I was pretty sure he had Empowerment in his BaZi. It was very clear by the look of his eyes. But this does not help me decide his hour of birth, as he already carried three Empowerments outside of his Hour Pillar. That said, with the three Empowerment on the Earthly Branch, I asked him how he felt about his career path. He replied that his career was not very smooth. With that, I assumed the Hour of E5 (Figure 66) was his hour of birth and started to analyze. It turned out to be quite a match with the events that happened to him that year, and eventually helped to solve a problem that troubled him a lot.

Why did I assume the Hour of E5 was his hour of birth? Because if he were born in Hour of E4, it would create a strong flow of Officer producing Empowerment, and his career path should be pretty smooth. His Grand Fortune started from the age of nine (starting from H7–E7). With the hour of birth confirmed, I was even able to tell that he majored in Science and Engineering, and switched career tracks to a managerial position at the age of 29. Those who are interested can try to analyze this case on their own.

In BaZi analysis, having the right hour of birth is very important. As a practice, I do not take cases when there is no way to tell the time of birth. The approaches I listed in this section, although all require skills and experiences, are still based on the fundamental principles of BaZi analysis. In practice, I would recommend starting by verifying the client's personality and derive further confirmation with the client's history and physical conditions if needed.

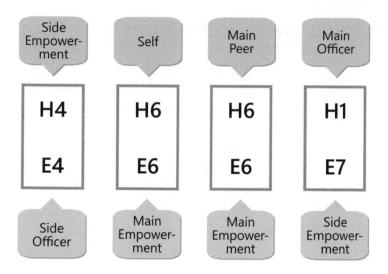

**Figure 65:** A possible BaZi Chart of a gentleman

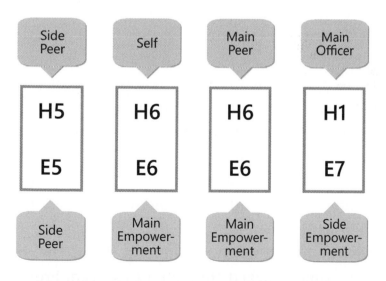

**Figure 66:** A possible BaZi Chart of a gentleman

# Section 5
# Picking a good time of birth

The concept of picking a time of birth may sound foreign to our English readers. In the Chinese-speaking world, however, it is quite common. Many parents would ask a practitioner of BaZi (or other forms of fortune-telling that is based on the person's time of birth) to pick a good date and time of birth and perform a Cesarean at the designated time.

When I was studying BaZi, whenever I heard of some celebrity that gave birth by Cesarean, I always checked the time of birth. I assume that many celebrities would pick a birth time for their children, and they often consult the most famous practitioners (or, at least, the most expensive ones). So the birth time they pick should be worthy of study.

But as I learned more, I realized that the chosen date and hour of birth, in many cases, were not ideal. In some cases, they stressed too much on one area and forgot others, or neglected the effect of coupling and transformation.

So how do we assist our clients if we were asked to pick a birth time for their children? Personally, I prefer a birth time that allows the BaZi to "flow smoothly." This means that the relationship amongst all the elements are predominantly production with as few countering as possible. Figure 17 is an example of a birth time I picked for a client. The child was born at the time I picked through a Cesarean. From what I know, the child is growing up in good health and has a very stable personality. I expect that he would have a smooth life as his BaZi indicates.

In practice, for parents who ask for help with birth time, I would pick a few options close to the expected delivery date, and show the possible personalities of each birth time with the BaZi it represents, so they can pick one they prefer. One must be very careful in an assignment like this. The selected BaZi needs to be checked and rechecked, making sure that everything is properly considered (including coupling and transformation). Unlike normal counseling sessions in which a client's BaZi is already fixed, our advice would determine the fate of a person that will stay with him throughout his entire life. If one is not sufficiently confident with his skill, it would be better off not taking such a request.

# Section 6
# Is it possible to predict one's time of marriage, time of death, and other major life events?

Can BaZi be used to predict one's major life events (getting married, having kids, buying a home, death, etc.)? This question is often asked and debated. Some believe that BaZi is useless unless it can predict these events.

From my experience, it is hard to tell exact timing through BaZi analysis. What the analysis can tell is the possibility of these events taking place during the given period. It is like the weather forecast, which can tell you that there is a storm ahead, but it cannot tell for sure that someone is going to be struck down by lightning.

When BaZi theory was first developed a thousand years ago, the society was a lot simpler, and the average life expectancy was a lot shorter. Most people got married between 12 and 18. It would have been a lot easier to predict when one would get married. The practitioner simply had to find the period with strong energy of Wealth for males and Officer for females between the ages of 12 and 20. Modern societies are a lot more complicated, and the possible age of marriage also gets a lot wider. Furthermore, in modern society, marriage is not the only form of relationship. The timing that we judge to be right for marriage could turn out to be the time that the person has started to date or move in with his/her partner, or even just engaged in a short-term romance.

It is the same for the time of death. With modern health care and medical technology, the traditional ways of predicting one's end of life no longer provide much value. What we can tell is the tides of energies across the years of our lives, and with that information, we take the best courses of action that will lead us to better health and fortune.

Many practitioners like to comment on the fortunes of the wealthiest or the most famous people, like Bill Gates or Warren Buffet. Most of them would comment as if these people had been destined to be so. In fact, we could almost certainly find someone with the same BaZi as these people (people who were born during the same hour of the same gender). They do not have the same wealth or fame (otherwise we would have known them). It is possible, however, that we can find similar patterns in these people, just at a much smaller scale. A man with the same BaZi as Barack Obama may not have been the first African American president of the United States, but he could be a charismatic leader and able to lead his community or organization. The magnitude of the achievement could be different, but there are similar patterns that can be found in them.

# Section 7
# Is one's life destined?

As a BaZi practitioner, I'm always asked whether I believe that everything that happens to a person is destined. I always tell them no. Then they would ask me what good BaZi is for if nothing is destined.

I do firmly believe that nothing is destined in life. Many fortune-tellers, including many traditional BaZi practitioners, promote the concept that everything is destined. This is not only confusing to those who seek to learn and get help from BaZi, but also rather fatalistic. Just think about it. Would it be possible that two persons with the same BaZi get married at the same time, have the same number of children, and die on the same day?

Furthermore, as compared to modern-day people, those who were born 300 years ago got married a lot younger, had more children, and lived shorter lives. All the fortune-telling systems, whether it is BaZi, tarot, or astrology, tell fortune just the same. How could they explain such differences?

What this tells us is that neither BaZi nor any fortune-telling method can give us the whole picture. Can BaZi tell us everything? My answer is no. Anyone who believes that a single fortune-telling method can predict everything would be superstitious. But does this mean that BaZi is useless? My answer is also no. My personal experience tells me that it is a very powerful tool. Even though, for example, the Dow Jones Index is used to analyze the stock market, it cannot tell you whether your investment will make money today, but it does not mean that it is useless. We cannot use BaZi to answer questions such as when a person is going to get married or how much money he is going to make, but we can get good indications that help us make better decisions at the right time.

So, can we change what is about to come? If BaZi analysis tells us that there is danger ahead, can we change it? The flow of energy is not something we can change. What we can do is to ride the flow. Try to put it to good use and avoid going against it. For example, during the period when the flow of energy indicates loss of wealth, we should avoid investing. We could instead ride the flow and spend some money on something useful (e.g., travel, education, charity). During the period of a potential accident, we do not engage in risky activities but could perhaps donate blood. It goes without saying that when the flow of energy goes in our favor, we should seize the opportunity and pursue our interests. In the next chapter, we will further discuss how to leverage and direct the flow of energy.

# Section 8
# The physics of BaZi

Those who have carefully studied the book up to this point should have been able to solve or analyze most BaZi cases. Here I want to discuss a more advanced and difficult principle—the physics of BaZi.

In the physical world, a force applied to an object may cause a certain effect, but the effect may not be immediate. A hammer slamming against a wall is not likely to make the wall fall in one strike. The wall could stand against many strikes and only falls after repeated strikes over a period time.

In BaZi analysis, we must also keep the same perspective as the law of physics. If a person sees H1 countering H5 over a period, does it mean that corresponding events could happen during this period? In most cases, something could happen, but sometimes it can be very minor or even unnoticeable. This is like the example of the hammer against the wall. The hammer strikes against the wall for some time. The wall may still hold and seems intact, but it could have been structurally damaged. Sometime later, a slight shake can bring the wall down.

Take one of my clients for example. She had serious H1 countering H5 in the later part of 2013. But nothing serious happened during that period. In late 2014 when H1 again countered H5, however, within a few weeks, she was diagnosed with cancer, which is related to countered Earth. The few short weeks of countering in 2014 cannot be the sole cause of cancer. It had to be related to the period during 2013. Also, the energy of H1 was enhanced in both 2012 and 2013. The cancer was most likely developed over the course of three years of countering.

Our skills of BaZi analysis could improve a lot if we could develop such a perspective of applying the laws of physics to our analysis. For example, if someone asks us whether it is appropriate to buy a house in a given month, not only do we have to check the flow of energy in that month, but we should also check the condition of the previous months or year. Take another example. A person who had just gone through a long period of Empowerment countering Creation should still watch out for the effect, despite the adverse flow of energy being gone, until the damaged Creation can be replenished by the energy of Peer.

Many important things in life are the result of continuous work over a long period. For example, the result of the bar examination for a law student is the result of her hard work over many years. The flow of energy during the month of the exam cannot tell the whole story. A good student with a bad energy flow during the month may not necessarily fail the exam. It is possible that he still passes the test with a score lower than expected. A student who never studies may not pass the exam even though the energy is in his favor. Hard work is always a major factor. The flow of energy, in most cases, simply moves it up or down a notch.

Those who analyze without taking into consideration the law of physics could be biased and become too absolute upon reading the signs at that moment. The world does not work that way. A good practitioner should not ignore continuous effects over time. To be able to incorporate such concepts and apply them to real cases, one has to be very proficient. This can only be achieved with lots and lots of practice.

# Chapter 7

# Debunking
# Common Myths
# and Superstitions

# Section 1
# The fallacy of the *fu-yi* (扶抑) method

As mentioned in the previous chapter, traditional BaZi analysis requires classifying the person's BaZi into strong/weak and dominative/submissive, then with it determine whether the person is Bodily Strong or Bodily Weak. Such a method is normally called Preferred Spirit (*xi yong shen* 喜用神) method or Supportive-Suppressive (*fu-yi* 扶抑) method. This method is, at best, not precise.

Sometimes, the clients I consult have learned a little bit of BaZi themselves. These people usually start the session by asking me whether they are Bodily Strong or Bodily Weak. Then they would go on to say that neither Bodily Strong nor Bodily Weak could well explain the things that happened in their lives. A few years ago, a client who lived in Hong Kong called me to discuss his BaZi. He had learned the traditional BaZi method himself. I told him that the energy of H1 was good for him, while H2 was bad. Furthermore, the energy of Wood on the Earthly Branch was side bad. He told me that is not how BaZi works. The energy of Wood either works in favor or against a person. Since both H1 and H2 are the energy of Wood, how could they cause different results? But after we discussed in detail and looked at his path of life, he conceded that my analysis was a lot more accurate and started to study my method.

There are a lot of similar cases. I had another client who is a physician. He is a very smart person and had studied the traditional BaZi method for years. But he still could not get a match with even the events in his own life. He searched in all the books he could find and studied cases with similar BaZi patterns as his. Still, he could not get it right. In our session, it took me only a few minutes to arrive at the results that he could not get in years. He was amazed.

The number of permutations of BaZi patterns is huge. The traditional classification of Strong/Weak and Dominative/Submissive is an oversimplification. Fitting such classification into millions of BaZi patterns inevitably results in lots of exceptions and mismatches. To cover these exceptions, the ancient BaZi researchers created exceptional patterns (such as the dominative pattern and submissive pattern we covered in Chapter 6). But these additional patterns created even more exceptions, and with that, more exceptional patterns were created. Many traditional BaZi books are full of different patterns, and in many cases, the patterns contradict one another. This is why we do not use it at all in our system. What we care about are the structure and composition of individual BaZi. The subtle and sophisticated interactions among the

Elements as well as with the external energy flow cannot be simply explained away with any crude method of classification.

With our system, we can analyze any BaZi pattern, including the rare patterns and new patterns we have never seen. I once wrote in an article that "the energy of Empowerment is good for the BaZi of submissive pattern if the chart is full of Officers." This completely contradicts the principle of traditional method, which says that a BaZi of submissive pattern is preferably under the energy of Creation, Officer, or Wealth. When I made such a comment, I had never seen any person with a BaZi full of Officers, so I made such a comment purely based on the principle of BaZi analysis. Then in May 2013, a lady came to seek my advice. In her BaZi, all elements except Self were Officers (four Main Officers and three Side Officers). A few years before our session, she had been working in China and made good money during the years of Empowerment. None of the BaZi practitioners she met before was able to get that right. But with my analysis, it was a perfect match.

So, why did our ancestors even develop such a seemingly useless framework? If we study it carefully, we could find that the framework, although overly simplified, is statistically not too far off. For example, those categorized as bodily weak usually have the strong energy of Officer. Under the energy of Empowerment, the energy of Officer can be directed to produce Empowerment, which brings a good flow of energy and fortune. The energy of Peer can enhance Creation, which suppresses the threat of Officers. In this sense, the traditional framework is correct. Nevertheless, if the person is strong with Wealth, then the presence of Peer is likely to signify the loss of wealth. The framework would be wrong in this case.

Is it always a good thing for a bodily strong person to be under the energy of Officer? If the person happens to have no Empowerment in his BaZi (or Empowerment is coupled), the presence of Officer can be a pretty bad sign.

There are other frameworks in traditional BaZi, such as *gong wei* (宮位) or *shen sha* (神煞). These frameworks simplify the sophisticated analytical process into a simple table lookup. They are highly inaccurate and contain lots of exceptions. But as they are easy to learn, many amateurs still use them. I have a student who had been studying all these frameworks for some years. Now he has quit those approaches altogether.

# Section 2
# Why some practitioners give wrong advice

Quite often my clients would ask me about their fortune with regards to their wealth during a specific year in the past. Interestingly, when that happens, I can almost be certain that they have lost money that year, and indeed that turned out to be true. Even more interestingly, when I told them my analysis, they would generally tell me that they had lost money that year because some practitioner told them they could have good fortune with regards to their wealth. This has happened time and again in my practice. The outcome of such bad advice could be very devastating. I have seen clients lose their retirement savings, and declaring bankrupt as a result.

All of these victims of bad advice asked me the same question: How can the advice from different BaZi practitioners be so drastically different? To answer their question, I spent a lot of time studying how other practitioners conduct their analysis. I found that there are many reasons that could create the wrong analysis and advice. A very common one is that the practitioners give their advice using incomplete information. For example, some practitioners only look at the presence of the Ten Spirits without analyzing the interactions among them. When Wealth is present, these practitioners would see it as a sign of good fortune with wealth, while in reality, it could be just the opposite (if the Wealth is countered by Peer). Analyzing using partial information is very dangerous. Presence of Wealth only means that matters related to Wealth may occur, but whether they are good or bad requires further analysis.

Here is one example that took place recently in my practice. This is a male client. His BaZi is shown in Figure 67. A few years ago, I foretold that when his Grand Fortune switched to E1 at the ages 48 to 53, he could have a problem with his marriage. It turned out that he indeed got divorced in August 2014. 2014 was the year of H1-E7. E7 is Main Wealth for him. Some practitioners may think that the presence of Main Wealth should enhance his luck with Wealth. If this is the case, he should not have divorced that year, as Wealth also symbolizes wife for a male. But in reality, under the influence of E1–E7 countering, the marriage of the client had been bad those years. The presence of E7 in 2014 enhanced the countering. This combined with H9 countering H4, and E9 enhancing E1 that countered E7. The marriage did not survive that month.

In fact, the condition could have been even worse in September 2014 (month of H10–E10), but the marriage ended before that. If the client could have been more patient and tolerant, things might have improved from December onwards. Also, the financial condition of the client was not well during those years.

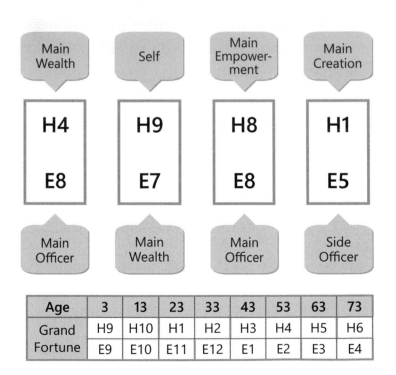

| Age | 3 | 13 | 23 | 33 | 43 | 53 | 63 | 73 |
|---|---|---|---|---|---|---|---|---|
| Grand | H9 | H10 | H1 | H2 | H3 | H4 | H5 | H6 |
| Fortune | E9 | E10 | E11 | E12 | E1 | E2 | E3 | E4 |

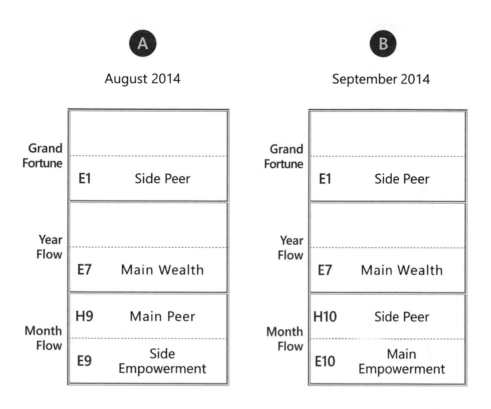

**Figure 67:** BaZi Chart of a male client

# Section 3
# Changing fortune

Quite a few practitioners claim that they can change a person's fortune through certain rituals. This indeed is quite appealing to many people. Many of my clients also asked me if I could help them change their fortune. The idea of being able to change one's fate for the better is very tempting, and many people would pay real money to give it a try. But personally, I believe that such a practice is pretty much a hoax, which changes nothing except lighten the weight of one's purse. I would like to advise readers not to fall for such ploys. If any practitioner claims that he can change your fortune with additional payment, stay away from him. Normally, such practitioners would paint your future as very grim to encourage you to pay extra (usually a very high price) for the "services." Many of them would even threaten or scare their clients by depicting great disasters ahead.

So, is it possible to change one's fortune? I believe so. Your thoughts decide your fortune, so as you change your thoughts, so does your fortune change. This is why we learn BaZi. We learn the flow of energy and how they work for us and incorporate it in our day-to-day lives as a guide to our actions and decisions. With a different attitude and course of action, one's fortune could be different even under the same flow of energy.

# Section 4
# The kinds of BaZi practitioners to keep away from

We have all heard of stories of fraud disguised as fortune-telling or religion. Victims suffer great losses. But it is human nature to seek guidance, especially during difficult or confusing times. So how do we choose the right counselor?

Since I started to learn BaZi and began my practice of counseling, I had the privilege of counseling many people. Since my book in Chinese was published a few years ago, many people from all walks of life came to me. I have counseled clients such as CEOs of public companies, university professors, medical doctors, high-tech industry executives, government officials, as well as carpenters, plumbers, social workers, housewives, and students. My clientele is quite diverse not just in occupation but also in background. It includes people of different sexual inclinations (homosexuals, heterosexuals, etc.), mental conditions (depression, bipolar, schizophrenia, etc.) as well as physical conditions. Face-to-face consultations with such diverse people have not only broadened my view and perspective of life and the world around me, but also helped me gain a deeper insight on the interpretation of BaZi and its effect on different people under different environments.

Another valuable but sad thing I learned from my clients is all the scams and schemes disguised under the name of fortune-telling, as many of them had first-hand experiences. On one hand, I am pleased with the fact that I was able to win the trust of my clients and that they are willing to share their personal experiences. On the other, I feel obliged to expose such scams so that people can take extra caution when they see it.

A common standard operating procedure of such scam or scheme looks like this:

1. Advertise fortune-telling consultation service for free or at a very low price.

2. During the session, practitioners would create a mental state of desire or fear in their clients. He could tell the client that he or she is destined to be a multimillionaire, and the only reason he or she is not living up to the destiny is that something got in the way. Alternatively, he could also tell the client that disaster will strike soon unless something is done. In either case, their purpose to make the client believe that they need a solution badly.

3. With that, the practitioners would go on to sell their "solution," which may be a talisman, a pendant that is "blessed," or some ritual to "change one's fortune." Not surprisingly, they charge an arm and a leg for these solutions.

The influence of such practice is so profound that I have so many clients who started the session by asking me to help them change their fortunes. In fact, the role of a consultant of BaZi or any type of fortune-telling is pretty much like a weather forecaster. He can tell the weather that lies ahead so you can adjust your actions, but he can never change the weather for you! If you encounter any practitioner suggesting that he can help you change your fate, just walk away! Don't even think of staying and hear what they have to say. These people are usually very good at pandering to your desire or fear. One could fall for it easily.

In addition to these apparent scams, there are many practitioners who do not have a solid understanding of BaZi. They may have learned a few vernaculars plus some frameworks, which are enough for them to act like a master in front of most clients. For them, BaZi is just a tool to make a living. They do not have a full understanding of BaZi and have no way of verifying their analysis. They tend to tell things in a way that is hard to verify, and needless to say, often misleading. Their analysis, even based on the same framework, can be all over the place. I have a client who showed me the analysis of the BaZi of his daughter from a few practitioners. Some analyzed her to be bodily strong while others bodily weak.

For most people, it is very hard to tell if a practitioner knows what he is doing or simply pretending. Here I share some common traits to pay attention to. If you see any of these, I advise you not to further waste your time or money.

- Those who keep mentioning *shen sha* (神煞)—*shen sha* is a set of names that sounds pretty mystical (in our English version I am not translating them. These names sound like those of tarots). It has been proven by most prominent BaZi masters that *shen sha* is not accurate at all. Most real practitioners have abandoned it altogether. But as these names sound mystical and intimidating, those who do not possess real skills still prefer to use it.

- Those who resort to zodiac animals—the zodiac is only related to the year of birth. Using only year of birth to tell one's fortune cannot be accurate. Those who say people of a certain zodiac sign is having a bad year (*fan tai sui* 犯太歲) cannot be a professional. It is even more ridiculous to tell whether a couple is good or bad for each other simply based on their zodiac signs.

- Those who analyze based on "Palaces" (*gong wei* 宮位)—the "Palace of Offspring," "Palace of Parents," and "Palace of Spouse" is yet another who is using a method that has been proven to be inaccurate. Moreover, the analysis is often highly subjective. Practitioners who use this method often come up with destructive advice. For example, they could advise parents to send their child away for adoption, or parents to live separately if they decide that they are not destined to be together.

- Those who talk about bodily strong and bodily weak—as we have covered previously, this framework is a rough estimate at best, with lots of exceptions. One should not entrust his destiny to the hands of such a crude framework.

- Those who do not distinguish yin and yang—yin and yang make a lot of difference in the results of the analysis. Practitioners who analyze the Five Elements without distinguishing yin from yang could derive wrong results.

All of the above methods that I advise against, the *shen sha*, the zodiac animals, the Palaces, the bodily strong and bodily weak, share something in common—they are all quite easy to learn. Although most of them employ lots of names that sound mysterious or even intimidating, in fact, they are little more than simple lookup tables, and the results are mostly binary. For amateurs or those who cannot perform the process of analysis, these simplified models are easy to learn. This might have been the reason that they have been so widely used. For professional counseling, however, these frameworks are not appropriate. The subject of life and destiny is among the most sophisticated subject, and it should not and cannot be explained away with one simple formula that yields only answers with a simple yes and no. Most of the books that cover these methods seem quite thick and are filled with seemingly serious discussions of cases. But if you read carefully, most of these discussions center around exceptional cases. A model based on a sound theory should not be full of exceptions.

With that, I urge you to stick to the principles that we have discussed in this book instead of those so-called "traditional" models. For one, they are not that "traditional" (the principle of yin/yang and the Five Elements have been around since the Han Dynasty, over 2000 years ago, while most of these frameworks have been around within only the last 300 years). More importantly, they have been proven to be inaccurate. Studying them is just like a modern-day chemist studying 16th century alchemy. It simply makes no sense.

# Chapter 8

# Practicing BaZi
# to Help Others:
# Some Advice

If you have spent a lot of effort studying this book, applying it on as many cases you can collect, and find that you can reach accurate results most of the time, chances are you will want to help more people with it. Although I do not choose to practice BaZi as my full-time career, throughout the years, I have used my BaZi analytical skills to help many people from all walks of life. In this chapter, I will share my experiences of how to best help others using BaZi.

## The right attitude of BaZi consultation

First of all, practice helping others ONLY if you are confident with your BaZi analytical skills. BaZi is an art of destiny. Wrong advice drawn from a flawed analysis could cause an adverse impact on the person's life. This is not something to be taken lightly. Moreover, if you are not confident and proficient in your skills, you may not have what it takes to respond to all the questions and challenges thrown at you by your client. How can someone trust you with his destiny if you cannot answer his questions with confidence?

Second, a heart that genuinely cares for the client is imperative. It is very important to listen to the client patiently and think carefully about the most diplomatic way to communicate. In most cases, try to deliver positive messages first. Many clients who come to seek help are experiencing some form of trouble or uncertainty. Telling them positive messages first can help improve their self-confidence, which they may lack at that moment. This could encourage them to face their challenge and to walk the path of their destiny with confidence.

On the other hand, be very sensitive when delivering the negative messages, such as the weaknesses of the person or possible negative events to come. Carefully phrase the message, so it does not cast a shadow in the heart of the client or make them panic. Usually, I would tell the client that life is like a boat in the ocean. It has its ups and downs, and sometimes good things happen in bad times, and bad things may happen in good times. For the period of bad luck that the client is currently or about to go through, I would tell them that it is only temporary and also tell them when the period will end, so they will not feel hopeless. Furthermore, I would also tell them that they still have control over their own lives. I am only helping them by pointing out the hazards and bad weather ahead. Bad things are not necessarily going to happen if they pay attention. And since they are aware of the dangers ahead, they will have an even better chance of avoiding serious damages.

Encouragement and positive phrases may help clients, but it does not help them solve the situation they are facing. Also, some clients are so troubled that they need more than encouraging words. Although we cannot change what lies ahead, there are certain ways to mitigate the situation. We are going to discuss this in the next section.

# Guiding the energy

Most readers should be familiar with the concept in physics called "conservation of energy." From all the cases I have studied, I found that this also applies to the energy of the Five Elements. When one type of energy strongly counters another, that countering has to manifest one way or another. Hiding from it or turning to religious rituals are not helpful. Instead, I would usually advise my clients to "guide" such energy into less harmful or even beneficial events. I call this "guiding the energy."

For example, if the analysis shows that the client may be subject to loss of wealth, then instead of losing money, why not spend it on something meaningful? Enrolling in a class and learning something new, taking a family vacation, and donating some money to charity all make a lot of sense.

In practice, we may provide some tips to guide the energy based on individual conditions (i.e., job, family condition, age) of the client. Here I am providing some simple examples of advice for clients under various adverse conditions. It would be even better if more detailed interactions among energies and coupling/transformation are taken into consideration.

- **Peer Countering Wealth:** we could advise the clients to avoid aggressive or high-risk investments during this period. Instead, guide the energy to healthy spending such as family trips or donations to charity. For male clients, we should also advise that they should pay more attention to caring for their spouse or girlfriend any to try to be more considerate.

- **Empowerment Countering Creation:** we should advise the clients to avoid making major decisions during this period, and pay extra attention not to be fooled or duped. They should also pay attention when driving to avoid accidents caused by a lapse of judgement. Think twice before speaking, especially in the workplace, or during important occasions to avoid making inappropriate comments.

- **Officers Countering Peers:** For Side Officer Countering Peers, clients should be advised not to engage in risky activities and to refrain from traveling. Also, advise the clients to pay attention to the possibility of being framed or backstabbed. As the energy of Side Officer is to restrain, torture, or even harm the person, some good ways to guide the energy include donating blood (self-inflicted harm that vents such energy) and strenuous exercise (self-inflicted torture).

- **Creation Countering Officer:** Advise clients to be more patient at the workplace, especially towards superiors. Wives should be more patient with their husbands.

- **Wealth Countering Empowerment:** Advise clients not to be overly aggressive in making money to avoid undesired consequences.

In addition to guiding adverse energies towards less harmful ways, we should also advise clients to take advantage of good energies coming their way:

- **Peer Producing Creation:** encourage clients to take the opportunity to make the best use of their talents, creating works, writing articles, proposing ideas, etc.

- **Creation Producing Wealth:** encourage clients to leverage their talents and ideas to create opportunities for generating wealth.

- **Officers Producing Empowerment:** encourage clients to take the opportunity to advance in their careers, get promotions or help from Noble Persons.

If needed, we may also suggest corresponding colors and directions based on the Five Elements that best help clients.

# Principle of confidentiality

Confidentiality must be upheld. A professional BaZi practitioner should assure his or her client that the entire process of the interview would be kept confidential. Even the visit itself will not be mentioned to anyone.

When I first tried to help my friends with BaZi, I was not aware of the importance of keeping the conversation discreet. I consulted with clients while others were waiting in the same room, and were able to listen to everything we discussed. Under such conditions, the clients will not likely open up and share their innermost secrets, which may be the real source of the problem.

# Fee

For a long time, I was unsure whether I should charge fees for consultation. Unlike those who make their living through fortune-telling, I do have a decent full-time job, and I only hope to help others with what I have learned. Charging a fee for offering help seemed a bit too utilitarian for me.

For those who are still practicing, each case provides a learning experience. Charging a fee may not be necessary or appropriate. For those who can already provide consultation with confidence, there are those who believe that fees must be charged, as "revealing the secret of destiny" is against the law of nature and can cause repercussions to the practitioner. Although this sounds superstitious, I think there is some practical reason behind such a belief.

Over the years, I have developed my own moral and practical standards on the matter of service fees. I believe that, as long as the practitioner is sufficiently professional and genuine in trying to help his or her clients get through difficulties in their lives, he or she should charge a reasonable consultation fee. This is not because the consultation may consume a lot of time and energy, but more importantly, human nature suggests that clients may not value the consultation if it is provided at no charge. People tend to take free consultations less seriously and may ask trivial, or even random questions as it costs them nothing. A reasonable fee could help ensure that only those who are serious about seeking help will come, and that those people will take the advice more seriously.

Hence I do suggest that any serious practitioner should charge a consultation fee, even if he or she does not do this for a living. The price, however, should be reasonable to those who do need help and can afford to seek it. Personally, for those who have financial difficulties, I would tell them to pay any amount they can afford. As a practice, I also donate a portion of the fee from each consultation to charity organizations.

# Skill, ethic, wisdom, opportunity

Last but not least, I believe that a professional practitioner should possess the qualities of "skill," "ethics," "wisdom," and "opportunity."

"Skill" means the skill to understand and analyze BaZi. The practitioner must be sufficiently proficient with the skills to provide real help to clients.

"Ethics" is critical. Clients who come to seek help are often at the most fragile moment of their lives. Taking advantage of their vulnerability is highly unethical. A real practitioner should give them a hand instead of taking advantage of them in their most desperate moment.

"Wisdom" decides how a practitioner enlightens the clients. Each client is different with different lives and worries. They may ask any question from any angle. If the practitioner is not equipped with sufficient knowledge, experience, and wisdom to properly respond, or if he practitioner does not appear confident or even comfortable in front of their client, then the consultation is pretty much a failure. Once the client loses trust in the practitioner, the practitioner can offer little help. A wise practitioner should always stick to the principles of BaZi theory, be careful in deducing answers, while not losing his or her confidence.

"Opportunity" means the right timing and condition. Not all who have learned BaZi and possesses all the previous three qualities have the opportunity to practice and help others. There is no need to feel disappointed if you cannot apply your skills. Maybe the timing has not arrived.

As a closing remark, I wrote this book not to promote my practice or myself. It is my intention that, through this book, readers can understand that BaZi is an art for everyone. Anyone can grasp the quintessence of the art of BaZi and apply it to help improve his or her life. It is also my hope that this book can help readers to build a correct appreciation of BaZi analysis, which is a logical process, regardless of any mythology or religion, so that our readers will not fall victim to scams disguised as truth in the name of BaZi. For those who have more questions or are interested in learning more, feel free to send me an email (prof.hwang.fortune.telling@gmail.com). I would be more than happy to hear from you.

Scan the above QR code to obtain my E-mail address.

The **Science** of
**Destiny Reading**
Using **BaZi** / Demystifying BaZi
the Logical Way

Authors: Gwan-Hwan Hwang Ph.D. / Hsing-Fen Chiang
Translator: Richard Wang
Proofreaders: Paul Choo / Helen Yeh

Cover Designer: Sha Yu Lin
Graphic Designer / Editor: Uncas

ISBN   978-986-318-765-3
Publication date: May 2019

Copyright © 2019 by Cosmos Culture Limited
Tel: +886-(0)2-2365-9739
Fax: +886-(0)2-2365-9835
Website: www.icosmos.com.tw
Email: onlineservice@icosmos.com.tw